EasyMeals
Rachel Allen

EasyMeals
Rachel Allen

Over 180 delicious recipes to get
you through your busy life

Collins

Contents

It seems like we all lead such hectic lifestyles these days. Even though I love to cook, often I just don't have the time to make complicated food. I'd love to spend six hours cooking an elaborate meal, but sometimes it just isn't realistic. I think that's true for a lot of people. Our lives are so busy now it can be difficult to set aside time to cook. That said, I don't think it's always the case that the more time you take over a meal the better it is. Truly great food can often be made in minutes and only using four or five ingredients.

It's not just time though; I often want fuss-free food for other reasons. Some days, for instance, I might cook a one-pot dish that bubbles away in the oven as I get on with other things. The other advantage of one-pot cooking is that with everything ready at the same time I don't have to coordinate various different side dishes. There are other times when I can't get to the shops so I need to make something using only ingredients that I already have at home. It is always so satisfying to be able to make good food using only things I can find in my cupboards, fridge or freezer, which means being able to use specific ingredients cleverly as well as knowing what things it's worth stocking up on.

This book is about times like these, when you want to cook a great meal but don't want lots of complex steps either in the preparation or in the actual cooking. That's why you'll find a chapter with recipes that use only five ingredients or fewer. I've also included a whole chapter for when you don't feel like turning on the oven at all. The recipes are unapologetically simple and straightforward – most are very quick from start to finish – yet they never compromise on flavour. A hectic lifestyle doesn't have to mean reaching for a sugary snack or ordering a takeaway. It's perfectly possible to cook wholesome food without too much time or fuss. This book shows you how to do just that – make food that is quick and simple yet always delicious.

Rachel x

PS. The oven temperatures in this book are for a conventional oven, but if I am using a fan oven then I usually reduce the temperature by 10 per cent.

Store Cupboard

We all have times when we need to create a meal using only what we have in the cupboard, fridge or freezer. To prepare for those times when you can't get to the shops, it's worth stocking up on basic ingredients with a long shelf-life. Tinned tomatoes and beans as well as dried pulses and pasta are perfect for such occasions. The recipes in this chapter also include meats such as bacon and leftover roast chicken, which I often have in my fridge. My freezer is usually full of things such as minced lamb or beef and, of course, peas. I sometimes keep a few long-life and versatile luxury foods too, such as dried porcini mushrooms or artichoke hearts preserved in oil.

It's not just savoury dishes that you can make with what you have on your shelves. Dry ingredients such as nuts, dried fruit and chocolate – both powdered and solid – make the store cupboard a treasure trove for baking and desserts.

Hearty lentil and onion soup

This is a rustic take on classic French onion soup. The lentils make it substantial and nutritious as well as bringing their own unique earthy flavour. The croutons are the perfect finishing touch, though you can make the soup without them if you prefer.

Serves 4 (v, if using vegetable stock)

PREPARATION TIME
10 minutes

COOKING TIME
1 hour

4 tbsp olive oil

6 onions (about 900g/2lb in total), peeled and finely sliced

Salt and freshly ground black pepper

150g (5oz) Puy lentils

3 tsp finely chopped rosemary leaves

1 litre (1¾ pints) chicken or vegetable stock

For the Gruyère croutons

4 slices of white bread

75g–100g (3–3½oz) Gruyère cheese, grated

* Pour the olive oil into a large saucepan on a medium heat and, when nearly hot, add the onions. Season with salt and pepper and cook, uncovered, for 25–30 minutes, stirring regularly and scraping the bottom of the pan to dislodge the caramelised pieces and mix them in, until the onions are a deep golden brown.

* Add the lentils, rosemary and stock. Bring to the boil then reduce the heat, cover with a lid and simmer for about 25 minutes or until the lentils are tender.

* Shortly before the soup is ready, preheat the grill to high to make the croutons (if using).

* Toast the bread on both sides, then cover each slice with a thick layer of grated cheese. Place back under the grill and toast until bubbling and melted.

* Season the finished soup with salt and pepper to taste and divide between bowls to serve. Place a whole crouton on top of each bowl of soup and add a grinding of black pepper. (If the slices of bread are too large, you may want to cut them into squares before serving.)

Rachel's tip

I always like to cook using extra virgin olive oil as I think it provides a divine depth of flavour. Throughout these recipes I've just called for olive oil but I recommend using extra virgin if you can, especially when used in a dressing.

Artichoke salad

Artichoke hearts in a tin or jar are one of the more luxurious preserved foods. Combined with semi-sun-dried tomatoes and preserved roasted red peppers, this is a really wonderful dish.

125g (4½oz) preserved artichoke hearts (from a jar or tin), cut into bite-sized pieces

75g (3oz) preserved roasted red peppers (from a jar or tin), cut into 2cm (¾in) dice

50g (2oz) semi-sun-dried tomatoes, roughly chopped

½ red onion, peeled and finely chopped

3 tbsp olive oil

2 tsp red wine vinegar

2 tsp pesto

Salt and freshly ground black pepper

Serves 4

PREPARATION TIME
5 minutes

* Simply mix everything together in a big bowl, season with salt and pepper to taste and serve.

Haricot bean and tuna salad

The intense flavours of sun-dried tomatoes and pesto can transform a tin of tuna into something really special. You can make this 2–3 hours ahead – store in the fridge until ready to serve.

4 tbsp chopped sun-dried tomatoes

2 x 400g tins of haricot beans, drained and rinsed

4 small spring onions, trimmed and sliced at an angle

120ml (4½fl oz) olive oil

2 tbsp red wine vinegar

2 tbsp pesto

2 x 185g tins of tuna, drained and broken into chunks

Salt and freshly ground black pepper

Serves 4–6

PREPARATION TIME
5 minutes

* In a bowl, mix together all the ingredients apart from the tuna, then carefully stir in the tuna, keeping it in chunks. Season with salt and pepper to taste and serve.

Perfect mushrooms on toast

I generally have a few mushrooms in my fridge – they are quick to cook and this is a great way of serving them. The anchovies dissolve in the butter, imparting a lovely depth of flavour to this dish.

Serves 4

PREPARATION TIME
10 minutes

COOKING TIME
20 minutes

110g (4oz) butter

12 tinned anchovies, chopped

6 cloves of garlic, peeled and sliced

800g (1¾lb) mushrooms, sliced

4 tsp chopped thyme leaves

Salt and freshly ground black pepper

4 slices of bread

25g (1oz) butter

100ml (3½fl oz) single or regular cream

* Melt the butter in a large frying pan on a medium heat and, when foaming, add the anchovies and garlic and cook, stirring frequently, for 2 minutes or until the anchovies have disintegrated and the garlic is lightly browned.

* Add the mushrooms and thyme, season with salt and pepper and reduce the heat to medium–low. Stir well, then cook, stirring occasionally, for 10–15 minutes or until the mushrooms are soft and browned.

* Meanwhile, toast the bread and butter it, then place on plates.

* Stir the cream into the mushrooms, increasing the heat to allow it to bubble for 1–2 minutes, then taste for seasoning and serve on the buttered toast.

Spiced baked eggs

Here's a slightly different way of serving eggs, and one that's incredibly easy, too. As the eggs cook gently in the oven, they take on the flavour of the spices and the silkiness of the cream. They're perfect with toast.

Serves 4 (v)

PREPARATION TIME
5 minutes

COOKING TIME
8–12 minutes

2 tsp ground cumin

½ tsp smoked paprika

Good pinch of cayenne pepper

4 eggs

Salt and freshly ground black pepper

4 tbsp single or regular cream

To serve

4 slices of bread

25g (1oz) butter

Four 100ml (3½fl oz) ramekins

* Preheat the oven to 200°C (400°F), Gas mark 6.

* In a small bowl, mix together the spices. Break each egg into a separate ramekin and sprinkle half the spice mixture over each egg. Season with salt and pepper, then add a tablespoon of cream to each dish.

* Place in the oven and cook for 8–12 minutes or until the white is just set and the yolk is still ever so slightly soft.

* Just before the eggs are ready, toast the bread and butter it, then remove the eggs from the oven and serve with the buttered toast.

Variation

Baked eggs with smoked mackerel: Divide 1 fillet of flaked smoked mackerel between the ramekins before adding the eggs, then proceed as above but omitting the spices.

Spiced beans and corn salsa toppings for baked potatoes

These toppings are a fabulous way of dressing up baked potatoes. They are also great with nachos or tortilla chips.

Each recipe serves 4 (v)

PREPARATION TIME
10 minutes each

COOKING TIME
15 minutes for the spiced beans topping

Spiced beans topping

2 tsp each coriander and cumin seeds

2 tbsp sunflower oil

2 onions, peeled and chopped

4 cloves of garlic, peeled and finely chopped

Salt and freshly ground black pepper

Pinch of cayenne pepper

2 x 400g tins of pinto, kidney or black beans

1 x 200g tin of chopped tomatoes

1 tsp caster sugar

* Toast and grind the coriander and cumin seeds. Place the seeds in a small frying pan on a high heat and cook, tossing frequently, for about 1 minute or until they are browned. Grind them into a powder with a pestle and mortar or place them in a plastic bag and use a rolling pin to crush them, then set aside.

* Pour the sunflower oil into a large frying pan on a medium heat. When hot, add the onions and garlic. Season with salt and pepper and stir occasionally for 10 minutes or until the onions are soft and lightly browned.

* Stir in the ground spices and the cayenne pepper and cook for 1 minute. Drain and rinse the beans and then stir them in. Season with salt and pepper and use your spoon to mash a few of the beans. Next, stir in the tomatoes and the sugar, bring to the boil, then reduce the heat and cook for 3 minutes or until the mixture is heated through. Taste for seasoning.

* Serve with baked potatoes and some crème fraîche or natural yoghurt, if you like.

Corn salsa topping

1 x 200g tin of sweetcorn

½ red onion, peeled and finely chopped

½ red or green chilli, deseeded and chopped

Juice of 1 lime

1 tbsp olive oil

* Drain and rinse the sweetcorn, then mix all the ingredients together and season to taste.

* Serve with baked potatoes, and some crème fraîche or natural yoghurt if you like.

Thai chickpea and mushroom curry

Green curry paste is an incredibly useful ingredient to have in your store cupboard – creating in an instant that subtle and complex balance of flavours that Thai food is all about. This delicious vegetable curry is substantial enough to serve on its own or with rice. To make it vegetarian, look for mock fish sauce, which is made from soy beans and often seaweed, or you can use soy sauce instead.

Serves 4

PREPARATION TIME
10 minutes

COOKING TIME
20 minutes

1 tbsp sunflower oil

250g (9oz) mushrooms, quartered

Salt and freshly ground black pepper

1–2 tbsp Thai green curry paste

1 tbsp soft dark brown sugar

1 x 400ml tin of coconut milk

1 x 400g tin of chickpeas, drained and rinsed

150g (5oz) potatoes, peeled and cut into 2–3cm (¾–1¼in) chunks

1 tbsp fish sauce (nam pla) or soy sauce for a vegetarian alternative

Juice of ½ lime

Chopped coriander, to serve (optional)

* Pour the sunflower oil into a large saucepan on a medium–high heat and, when hot, add the mushrooms, season with salt and pepper and cook for 8–10 minutes or until the mushrooms are golden.

* Stir in the curry paste and sugar, then stir in the coconut milk. Season with salt and add the chickpeas and potatoes.

* Bring to a simmer and cook for 8–10 minutes or until the potatoes are soft, then stir in the fish sauce or soy sauce and lime juice. Serve immediately with a sprinkling of fresh coriander (if using).

Tarka dahl

Dahl is a traditional and simple Indian dish made from lentils. Red lentils are such a useful ingredient to have in your store cupboard. They are full of nutrients, easy to cook and have a glorious nutty flavour that can be enhanced by different spices.

Serves 4–6 (v)

PREPARATION TIME
5 minutes

COOKING TIME
15 minutes

400g (14oz) red lentils

8 slices of peeled root ginger 5mm (¼in) thick

1 bay leaf

50g (2oz) butter

10 cloves of garlic, peeled and finely sliced

4 tsp cumin seeds

1 tsp dried chilli flakes

Salt and freshly ground black pepper

* Place the lentils in a saucepan, along with the ginger, bay leaf and 1.5 litres (2½ pints) water. Bring to the boil, then reduce the heat and simmer for 10–15 minutes, skimming off and discarding any foam that rises to the surface, until the lentils are soft.

* While the lentils are cooking, melt the butter in a small frying pan on a medium–high heat. When the butter starts to foam, add the garlic, cumin and chilli flakes and stir-fry for 1–2 minutes or until the garlic is lightly browned.

* Serve the cooked lentils on a bed of boiled rice (see page 332) with the garlic butter poured over the top and seasoned with salt and pepper.

Poached eggs with bacon lentils

I can usually find lentils lurking somewhere in my store cupboard, and by adding bacon and serving them with poached eggs, they make a really substantial lunch or supper.

Serves 4

PREPARATION TIME
5 minutes

COOKING TIME
25 minutes

4 eggs

Splash of vinegar

4 tbsp chopped parsley (optional)

For the bacon lentils

4 tbsp olive oil

200g (7oz) bacon (in the piece or about 6 rashers), cut into 2cm (¾in) dice

300g (11oz) Puy lentils

1 bay leaf

1 sprig of rosemary

Salt and freshly ground black pepper

* First make the bacon lentils. Pour half the olive oil into a large saucepan on a medium heat and, when hot, add the bacon and fry for 6–8 minutes or until crispy.

* Add the lentils, bay leaf and rosemary to the pan with 500ml (18fl oz) water. Bring to the boil, then reduce the heat and simmer for about 15 minutes or until the lentils are soft. Drain off any excess water and discard the bay leaf and rosemary, then stir in the remaining olive oil and season with salt and pepper.

* Five minutes before the lentils are ready, poach the eggs. Place a saucepan of water on a high heat, add a splash of vinegar and bring to the boil. Reduce the heat to a simmer, gently crack in the eggs and cook for 3–4 minutes or until the whites have just set.

* To serve, divide the lentils between plates, then carefully remove the eggs from the pan with a slotted spoon and place on top of the lentils. Season with salt and pepper to taste and sprinkle over the chopped parsley (if using).

Instant dips

Store cupboard ingredients are ideal for making dips, allowing you to have everything ready in minutes. Mixing the bean and the red pepper dips by hand is almost as quick as using a processor.

Each recipe serves 4 (v)

PREPARATION TIME
5 minutes each

Bean dip

1 x 400g tin of white beans, such as haricot or cannellini, drained and rinsed

1 clove of garlic, peeled and crushed or finely grated

1 tsp chopped rosemary leaves

75ml (3fl oz) olive oil

Salt and freshly ground black pepper

* Whiz everything together in a food processor for 3–4 minutes or until smooth. Alternatively, mash the beans with a fork or potato masher and mix in the remaining ingredients. Add salt and pepper to taste and serve.

Red pepper and chickpea dip

1 x 400g tin of chickpeas, drained and rinsed

275g (10oz) preserved all s

3 tbsp olive oil

Salt and freshly ground black pepper

* Place all the ingredients in a food processor together with 2 tablespoons of water and whiz for 3–4 minutes or until smooth. Alternatively, mash the chickpeas with a fork or potato masher and finely chop the red peppers, then mix with the olive oil. Add salt and pepper to taste and serve.

Sun-dried Tomato dip

200g (7oz) semi-sun-dried tomatoes

2 tbsp olive oil

1 clove of garlic, peeled and crushed or finely grated

25g (1oz) pine nuts

Salt and freshly ground black pepper

* Whiz everything together in a food processor for 3–4 minutes or until smooth. Add salt and pepper to taste and serve.

Huevos rancheros

This is a classic Mexican breakfast dish – eggs surrounded by a sweet-tasting mixture of red peppers and tomato – but you can eat it at any time of day. It's great as it is or served with tortillas and guacamole or sliced avocado.

Serves 2–4 (v)

PREPARATION TIME
10 minutes

COOKING TIME
25 minutes

25g (1oz) butter

2 red onions, peeled and finely chopped

1 red pepper, deseeded and cut into 1cm (½in) dice

2 cloves of garlic, peeled and finely chopped

Good pinch of cayenne pepper

2 tsp ground cumin

Salt and freshly ground black pepper

1 x 400g tin of chopped tomatoes

Good pinch of granulated or caster sugar

4 eggs

25g (1oz) Cheddar cheese

* Melt the butter in a large frying pan on a medium heat and, when foaming, add the onions, red pepper, garlic, cayenne pepper and cumin and season with salt and pepper. Cook, stirring occasionally, for 8–10 minutes or until the onions and pepper are soft and lightly browned.

* Stir in the tomatoes and sugar and cook for about 5 minutes or until the liquid has reduced a little.

* Use a spoon to make 4 wells in the mixture, then break an egg into each of the 4 spaces. Season with salt and pepper, cover the pan with a lid and cook for 3–4 minutes or until just set.

* Grate over the cheese, replace the lid on the pan for a few seconds, then serve.

Smoked salmon and chive fish cakes

With their crisp outer coating, soft fluffy mash and delicate flakes of smoked salmon, these fish cakes are a supremely comforting food.

Makes 6 fish cakes

PREPARATION TIME
15 minutes

COOKING TIME
50 minutes

500g (1lb 2oz) floury potatoes, unpeeled and scrubbed clean

Salt and freshly ground black pepper

225g (8oz) smoked salmon

3 tbsp olive oil

1 red onion, peeled and finely chopped

2 tbsp finely chopped chives

1 tbsp capers, drained and chopped

Good squeeze of lemon juice

1 egg, beaten

75g (3oz) breadcrumbs

15g (½oz) butter

* Preheat the oven to 220°C (425°F), Gas mark 7 and grease a small baking tray with olive oil.

* Fill a large saucepan with water, then add the potatoes and a good pinch of salt. Bring to the boil for 10 minutes, then pour all but about 4cm (1½ in) of the water out of the pan and cook the potatoes on a very low heat for another 20–30 minutes until a skewer goes in easily. Peel them while they are still hot and mash immediately, either by hand or using the paddle attachment in an electric food mixer, until they are free of lumps.

* Meanwhile, as the potatoes cook, place the smoked salmon on the baking tray. If it is pre-sliced, simply put the slices one on top of the other. Drizzle the salmon with 1 tablespoon of the olive oil, then bake in the oven for 6–8 minutes. Remove from the oven and set aside.

* Put the mashed potato, onion, chives, capers, lemon juice, egg and breadcrumbs into a large mixing bowl. Roughly tear the smoked salmon into smaller pieces and add to the mix. Use a spoon to stir everything together – the salmon will break up further as you mix. Season with salt and pepper.

* Shape the mixture in to six patties, each about 8cm (3in) wide and 2cm (¾ in) thick. The uncooked fish cakes can be prepared up to this point in advance and either frozen or kept in the fridge for up to 24 hours.

* To cook, pour the remaining 2 tablespoons of olive oil into a large frying pan on a medium heat and add the butter. When the butter has melted and starts to foam, add the fish cakes and fry for 3–5 minutes on each side or until golden brown and crispy. Serve with a green salad, lemon wedges and a dollop of tartare sauce or mayonnaise.

Spaghetti with anchovies, garlic and chilli

This is a great simple pasta dish with strong punchy flavours. Dried chilli flakes can be quite hot, so just add a small pinch if you prefer less of a kick.

Serves 4

PREPARATION TIME
10 minutes

COOKING TIME
10–12 minutes

Salt and freshly ground black pepper

350g (12oz) dried spaghetti or other pasta, such as linguine or tagliatelle

4 tbsp olive oil

6–8 cloves of garlic, peeled and sliced

10 tinned anchovies, chopped

1–2 pinches of dried chilli flakes

2 tbsp chopped parsley

Good squeeze of lemon juice

* Fill a large saucepan with water, add 1 teaspoon of salt and bring to the boil. Add the spaghetti and cook for 10–12 minutes or according to the instructions on the packet, until al dente.

* As the pasta is cooking, place another saucepan on a medium heat. (The pan should be large enough to hold all of the spaghetti once it is cooked.) Add the olive oil, followed by the garlic, and fry for 2 minutes, then stir in the anchovies and chilli flakes and cook for a further minute.

* Drain the spaghetti, reserving some of the cooking liquid, then add to the anchovy mixture with a few tablespoons of the liquid. Tip in the chopped parsley, stir to mix, then add the lemon juice. Taste, adding a further squeeze of lemon if you like. Add a grinding of black pepper and serve immediately.

Fusilli with tuna, capers and cream

A tin of tuna and some pasta are enough to make a meal, though for added interest I've included capers and garlic. You can also stir in a few chopped olives, if you wish.

Serves 4

PREPARATION TIME
5 minutes

COOKING TIME
10–12 minutes

Salt and freshly ground black pepper

350g (12oz) dried fusilli, or other pasta shape such as penne or farfalle

3 cloves of garlic, peeled and crushed or finely grated

3 tbsp capers, drained and rinsed

100ml (3½fl oz) single or regular cream

2 x 185g tins of tuna, drained and broken into chunks

3 spring onions, trimmed and sliced at an angle

* Fill a large saucepan with water, add 1 teaspoon of salt and bring to the boil. Add the fusilli and cook for 10–12 minutes or according to the instructions on the packet, until al dente.

* While the fusilli is cooking, mix together the other ingredients in a bowl, seasoning with salt and pepper to taste. When the pasta is cooked, drain it, then stir into the tuna mixture and serve.

Tinned-tomato pasta

This is a classic tomato sauce using tinned tomatoes with zingy additional flavour from garlic, olives and capers. Adding sugar is important as tinned tomatoes don't have the sweetness of fresh tomatoes in summer.

Serves 4

PREPARATION TIME
5 minutes

COOKING TIME
10–12 minutes

Salt and freshly ground black pepper

300g (11oz) dried pasta, such as spaghetti, fusilli, penne, tagliatelle or linguine

6 tbsp olive oil

2 onions, peeled and finely chopped

4 cloves of garlic, peeled and crushed or finely grated

4 tsp chopped capers

About 10 black olives, pitted and chopped (optional)

2 x 400g tins of chopped tomatoes

2 tsp granulated or caster sugar

50g (2oz) Parmesan cheese, grated

* Fill a large saucepan with water, add 1 teaspoon of salt and bring to the boil. Add the pasta and cook for 10–12 minutes or according to the instructions on the packet, until al dente.

* Meanwhile, place another saucepan on a medium heat. (The pan should be large enough to hold all the pasta once it is cooked.) Add the olive oil, followed by the onions and garlic, then season with salt and pepper and cook, stirring occasionally, for 6–8 minutes or until the onions are softened and lightly coloured.

* Stir in the capers and olives (if using), cook for a further minute, then stir in the chopped tomatoes and sugar. Continue to cook for another 3 minutes, then drain the pasta and add to the pan with the sauce. Mix together, then divide between bowls and serve with freshly grated Parmesan cheese.

Tagliatelle with bacon, peas and mint

Long thin pastas are perfect for creamy sauces, with each strand evenly coated. Spaghetti works here, too, but for this dish I prefer the texture and slightly chunkier shape of tagliatelle.

Serves 4

PREPARATION TIME
5 minutes

COOKING TIME
10–12 minutes

Salt and freshly ground black pepper

350g (12oz) dried tagliatelle or other pasta, such as spaghetti or linguine

2 tbsp olive oil

200g (7oz) streaky bacon (about 8 rashers), rind removed and cut into 2cm (¾in) dice

300ml (½ pint) single or regular cream

200g (7oz) frozen peas

2 tbsp chopped mint

50g (2oz) Parmesan cheese, finely grated

* Fill a large saucepan with water, add 1 teaspoon of salt and bring to the boil. Add the tagliatelle and cook for 10–12 minutes or according to the instructions on the packet, until al dente.

* While the pasta is cooking, pour the olive oil into a large saucepan on a medium–high heat and, when hot, add the bacon. (The pan should be large enough to hold the tagliatelle when it is cooked.) Fry for about 5 minutes or until the fat has rendered and the bacon is golden and crispy.

* Stir in the cream and allow to bubble for a couple of minutes, then stir in the peas and keep cooking for a minute or two more or until they are just tender. Remove from the heat, then drain the tagliatelle and add to the sauce, stirring it in along with the chopped mint.

* Taste for seasoning and serve with the Parmesan cheese sprinkled over the top.

Chicken and bacon pilaf

With just a little fried onion and some stock you can transform boiled rice into a really tasty dish. The chicken and bacon makes this a substantial meal. If you have some fresh herbs, stir them in for extra flavour.

Serves 4–6

PREPARATION TIME
10 minutes

COOKING TIME
30–35 minutes

4 tbsp olive oil

300g (11oz) streaky bacon (in the piece or about 10 rashers), rind removed and cut into 2cm (¾in) dice

25g (1oz) butter

1 onion, peeled and finely chopped

300g (11oz) basmati rice

800ml (1 pint 9fl oz) chicken stock

Salt and freshly ground black pepper

200g (7oz) frozen peas

300g (11oz) cooked chicken (or see tip), cut into bite-sized pieces

* Pour the olive oil into a large saucepan on a medium heat and, when hot, add the bacon and fry for 6–8 minutes or until the fat has rendered and the bacon is golden and crispy. Remove the bacon from the pan and set aside, retaining any oil left in the pan.

* Melt the butter in the saucepan with the bacon fat, then add the onion and cook for 6–8 minutes or until soft and lightly browned.

* Next, add the rice and stock, season with salt and pepper, then bring to the boil, reduce the heat and simmer for about 14 minutes or until the rice is soft and fluffy. Stir in the peas, fried bacon and chicken and cook for a further minute, then taste for seasoning and serve.

Rachel's tips

Butchers and some supermarkets will sell bacon 'in the piece'. This is often better for cooking with than rashers, because rather than thin pieces you can get nice juicy chunks.

If you don't have leftover cooked chicken, then just poach some in the stock – it hardly takes any time. Cut an uncooked skinless chicken breast into bite-sized pieces, bring the stock to the boil in a saucepan, then season with salt and pepper and add the chicken to the pan. Bring back up to the boil and poach for about 5 minutes or until the chicken is opaque all the way through. Remove the chicken, then use the stock to cook the rice as above, before stirring in the cooked chicken with the peas and bacon.

Bacon and potato gratin

A bubbling, golden crispy potato 'lid' hides more layers of soft and creamy potato beneath. This comforting dish is so simple to put together that it's a great example of how just a few ingredients can combine to produce something really special.

Serves 6–8

PREPARATION TIME
15 minutes

COOKING TIME
1½ hours

2 tbsp olive oil

375g (13oz) bacon (in the piece or about 10 rashers), cut into 1–2cm (½–¾in) dice

1 onion, peeled and finely chopped

2 cloves of garlic, peeled and finely chopped

1 tbsp chopped thyme leaves

Salt and freshly ground black pepper

1kg (2lb 3oz) potatoes, peeled and cut into 5mm (¼in) thick slices

300ml (½ pint) single or regular cream

50g (2oz) Gruyère or Cheddar cheese, grated (optional)

2 litre (3½ pint) gratin or ovenproof dish

* Preheat the oven to 200°C (400°F), Gas mark 6.

* Pour the olive oil into a frying pan on a medium heat and, when hot, add the bacon and fry for about 5 minutes or until crispy. Stir in the onion, garlic and thyme, season with salt and pepper (bearing in mind that the bacon is quite salty) and cook for a further 6–8 minutes or until the onion is soft and a little golden.

* Meanwhile, arrange half of the potato slices in the gratin or ovenproof dish, season with salt and pepper, then spread over the cooked bacon and onion. Arrange the remaining potatoes over the top and season again with salt and pepper.

* Pour over the cream. Add the grated cheese (if using) in a layer on top, then cover with foil and place in the oven. Bake for 45 minutes, then remove the foil and return to the oven for a further 30–35 minutes or until lightly browned and crispy on top.

Baked mushroom risotto

Dried porcini mushrooms are a magical food. Soaked in water they release an intense, almost beefy aroma. The soaking liquid then flavours the rice and enhances the taste of the other mushrooms in the recipe.

Serves 4–6

PREPARATION TIME
**15 minutes,
plus soaking**

COOKING TIME
45 minutes

**50g (2oz) dried porcini
mushrooms**

**400ml (14fl oz) boiling
water**

**125g (4½oz) butter,
softened**

**2 onions, peeled and
finely chopped**

**4 cloves of garlic, peeled
and finely chopped**

**800ml (1 pint 9fl oz)
chicken or vegetable
stock**

**Salt and freshly ground
black pepper**

400g (14oz) risotto rice

200ml (7fl oz) white wine

**500g (1lb 2oz) flat
mushrooms, sliced**

**8 tbsp freshly grated
Parmesan cheese, plus
extra to serve**

**4 tbsp chopped marjoram
or parsley**

Squeeze of lemon juice

**1–2 tbsp mascarpone
(optional)**

* Place the porcini mushrooms in a heatproof bowl, pour over the boiling water and leave for 20 minutes until soft.

* Preheat the oven to 180°C (350°F), Gas mark 4.

* Melt 25g (1oz) of the butter in a large casserole dish or ovenproof saucepan on a medium heat. Add the onions and garlic and sauté for 6–8 minutes or until soft and turning golden. Meanwhile, pour the stock into a separate pan, bring to the boil, then reduce the heat and leave to simmer on the hob.

* While the onions are cooking, drain the porcini mushrooms, reserving the soaking liquid. Roughly chop the mushrooms and set aside, then strain the soaking liquid (to remove any sand or grit) and add to the simmering stock. Season this liquid with salt and pepper.

* Add the chopped porcini mushrooms to the onions and cook, stirring frequently, for 1–2 minutes. Next, tip in the rice and gently stir-fry for a further 2 minutes.

* Pour in the wine, then bring to a simmer, stirring as the mixture heats up, and cook for 2–3 minutes or until the wine has evaporated. Pour in the simmering stock, stirring to combine, then bring to the boil, cover and bake in the oven for 10–12 minutes or until just al dente.

* Meanwhile, melt 25g (1oz) of the butter in a frying pan on a medium heat, add the flat mushrooms and fry, stirring occasionally, for 3–5 minutes or until softened and lightly golden. Remove from the heat and set aside.

* Remove the risotto from the oven and add the grated Parmesan cheese and remaining 75g (3oz) butter, then use a wooden spoon to vigorously beat everything together. Stir in the fried mushrooms, along with the marjoram or parsley, lemon juice and mascarpone (if using). Serve immediately with extra Parmesan on top.

Tomato and rosemary risotto with meatballs

You can serve the risotto on its own, although the meatballs turn a light dish into a hearty meal. The meatballs can be stored in the freezer (before cooking), but defrost them fully before frying.

Serves 4–6

PREPARATION TIME
**15 minutes,
plus chilling**

COOKING TIME
25–30 minutes

450g (1lb) beef or pork mince

1 tsp chopped thyme

5 cloves of garlic, peeled and crushed

1 egg, beaten

Salt and freshly ground black pepper

4–5 tbsp olive oil

1 onion, peeled and finely chopped

400g (14oz) risotto rice

150ml (5fl oz) white wine

2 x 400g tins of chopped tomatoes

2 tsp caster sugar

1 litre (1¾ pints) chicken or vegetable stock

3 tsp chopped rosemary

25g (1oz) butter, diced

150g (5oz) Parmesan cheese, finely grated, plus extra to serve

* First make the meatballs. Place the mince in a bowl with the thyme, just over half the garlic and the beaten egg, season with salt and pepper and mix well together. To check the seasoning, fry 1 teaspoon of the mixture in a frying pan for 1–2 minutes or until cooked through. Taste to see whether you need to add more salt or pepper to the mixture.

* Using wet hands, form the mixture into 16–20 tiny little meatballs, each about 2cm (¾in) in diameter, then chill (for up to 24 hours) until you are ready to cook them.

* Preheat the oven to 180°C (350°F), Gas mark 4.

* Next, make the risotto. Pour 3 tablespoons of the olive oil into an ovenproof saucepan on a low–medium heat and, when hot, add the onion and garlic and season. Cook for 7–8 minutes or until soft and a little golden.

* Add the rice, increase the heat to medium and cook for 1–2 minutes or until it starts to crackle. Pour in the wine and allow to bubble until the liquid has evaporated. Tip in the tomatoes and sugar, bring to the boil, then reduce the heat and cook for 3–4 minutes or until almost soft. Add the stock and half the rosemary, bring back to the boil, cover with a lid and bake for 10–12 minutes.

* While the risotto is cooking, fry the meatballs. Pour the remaining olive oil into a large frying pan on a medium heat and, when hot, add the meatballs and fry for 10–12 minutes, turning regularly, until evenly browned and cooked through. Remove from the heat and set aside.

* Remove the risotto from the oven and beat in the butter and most of the Parmesan cheese with a wooden spoon. Taste for seasoning, then divide between bowls, top with the meatballs and sprinkle over the remaining Parmesan.

Spiced lamb pittas

This deliciously spicy mince mixture tastes wonderful served with lightly toasted pitta breads and a few spoonfuls of Greek yoghurt. Use beef mince instead of lamb if that's what you have to hand, it's still delicious.

Serves 4–6

PREPARATION TIME
10 minutes

COOKING TIME
20–25 minutes

2 tbsp olive oil

1 onion, peeled and chopped

1 large clove of garlic, peeled and crushed or finely grated

Salt and freshly ground black pepper

1 tsp turmeric

1 tsp ground cumin

1 tsp ground coriander

450g (1lb) lamb mince

225g (8oz) potatoes, peeled and cut into 5mm (¼in) dice

75g (3oz) frozen peas

To serve

4–6 pitta breads

About 150ml (5fl oz) natural Greek yoghurt

* Pour the olive oil into a large frying pan on a high heat and, when hot, add the onion and garlic and season with salt and pepper. Fry, stirring frequently, for 6–8 minutes or until the onion is cooked and golden at the edges.

* Add the spices and mince and cook for 4–5 minutes or until the mince loses its raw colour. Tip in the potatoes and 50ml (2fl oz) water, then cover with a lid, reduce the heat to medium and simmer for 8–10 minutes or until the potatoes are just tender, then add the peas and cook, uncovered, for a further 2 minutes.

* Shortly before the spiced mince is ready, toast the pitta breads and pour the Greek yoghurt into a small serving bowl. Season the cooked lamb to taste and serve with the toasted pittas and yoghurt.

Lamb meatballs

These delicately aromatic meatballs are very happy resting on a bed of couscous – a seriously useful store cupboard ingredient that is ready to serve after only a few minutes soaking in stock or hot water (see page 333). The meatballs can be stored in the freezer before cooking (defrost them well before use).

Serves 4–6

PREPARATION TIME
**10 minutes,
plus chilling**

COOKING TIME
10–15 minutes

6 green cardamom pods

500g (1lb 2oz) lamb mince

Finely grated zest of 1 lemon

1 onion, peeled and grated

2 cloves of garlic, peeled and crushed or finely grated

Salt and freshly ground black pepper

2 tbsp olive oil

For the sauce:

200ml (7fl oz) natural Greek yoghurt

1 tsp turmeric

Juice of 1 lemon

1 cucumber, cut into 2cm (¾in) chunks (optional)

* Place the cardamom pods on a chopping board, lay the flat side of a large knife over the top and press down to lightly crush. Remove the seeds (discarding the pods) and crush to a powder with a pestle and mortar or place in a plastic bag and use a rolling pin to crush them.

* Place the crushed seeds in a bowl with the lamb mince, lemon zest, onion and garlic, then season with salt and pepper and mix together. To check the seasoning, fry 1 teaspoon of the mixture in a frying pan for 1–2 minutes or until cooked through, then taste to see whether you need to add more salt or pepper to the mixture.

* Using wet hands, form the mixture into 20–24 meatballs, each about 3–4cm (1¼–1½in) in diameter, then leave to chill in the fridge (for up to 24 hours) until you are ready to cook them.

* Pour the olive oil into a frying pan on a medium heat and, when hot, add the meatballs and fry them for 8–12 minutes, tossing occasionally, until well browned and cooked through.

* To make the sauce, simply mix all the ingredients together in a bowl. Season to taste with salt and pepper. Serve drizzled over the meatballs on a bed of couscous (see page 333).

Chocolate, toffee and peanut squares

One of my guilty pleasures is a tin of boiled condensed milk. The sugars in the milk caramelise to make a thick toffee-like sauce. It's perfect for cooking or eating straight from the tin (with or without a spoon!). It's also possible to buy ready-boiled condensed milk, which is sold in jars as dulce de leche. If you want to make your own, boil unopened tins of condensed milk for 2 hours – I like to prepare a few tins at a time and then keep them in the cupboard where they'll store for months.

**Makes about
24 squares** (v)

PREPARATION TIME
10 minutes

COOKING TIME
**20 minutes,
plus chilling**

100g (3½oz) caster sugar

**200g (7oz) butter,
softened and diced**

**300g (11oz) self-raising
flour, sifted**

**400ml (14fl oz) dulce
de leche or boiled
condensed milk (see
recipe introduction,
above)**

**125g (4½oz) salted
peanuts, roughly chopped**

**200g (7oz) milk
chocolate, broken into
pieces**

*20 x 30cm (8 x 12in)
Swiss roll tin*

* Preheat the oven to 180°C (350°F), Gas mark 4. Line the base of the Swiss roll tin with baking parchment.

* In a food processor, whiz together the sugar, butter and flour for the shortbread base until the mixture resembles coarse breadcrumbs. Alternatively, rub together the butter and flour in a bowl with your fingertips and stir in the sugar. Tip into the prepared tin and press down with your hands or a palette knife to level out the mixture.

* Place in the oven and bake for about 20 minutes or until golden brown all over, then remove from the oven and allow to cool in the tin.

* Once it is cool, spread over the dulce de leche to cover the shortbread, then press the roughly chopped peanuts into it, making sure they are evenly distributed.

* Place the chocolate in a heatproof bowl set over a saucepan of simmering water and allow to melt. Remove from the heat and pour over the peanut-studded dulce de leche, allowing it to cool, then leave in the fridge for 1–2 hours to set. Once set, cut the mixture into squares in the tin and serve.

Easy lemon cake

As the title of this recipe suggests, this cake is ridiculously simple to make. It's just a matter of whizzing all the ingredients together in a food processor before tipping the mixture into a tin and baking in the oven. If you don't have a food processor, it's still very easy to make by hand and tastes just as delicious, either way!

Serves 4–6 (v)

PREPARATION TIME
10 minutes

COOKING TIME
30–35 minutes

110g (4oz) butter,
softened and diced

110g (4oz) caster sugar

Finely grated zest of
½ lemon

2 eggs

150g (5oz) plain flour,
sifted

½ tsp baking powder

1 tbsp milk

For the icing

175g (6oz) icing sugar

2–3 tbsp lemon juice

*20cm (8in) diameter
spring-form/loose-
bottomed cake tin*

* Preheat the oven to 180°C (350°F), Gas mark 4. Line the base of the tin with a disc of baking parchment and grease the sides with butter.

* Place all the ingredients for the cake in a food processor and whiz for 1 minute or just until the mixture comes together. Alternatively, cream the butter until soft using a hand-held electric beater, then beat in the sugar and lemon zest, whisk in the eggs one at a time and fold in the remaining ingredients. Tip the mixture into the prepared tin, smoothing over the top with a palette knife or the back of a spoon.

* Place in the oven and bake for 30–35 minutes or until golden on top and a skewer inserted into the centre of the cake comes out clean. Leave to stand for 5 minutes before removing from the tin and placing on a wire rack to cool.

* To make the icing, sift the icing sugar into a bowl and add just enough lemon juice to make a soft icing with the consistency of thick double cream. (Too thick and it won't 'self-spread', too thin and it will run off the cake and onto the plate beneath.)

* Place the cake on a serving plate and tip the icing into the middle of the cake, allowing it to spread itself, then cut into slices to serve.

Rachel's tip

If the icing is a bit stiff and won't spread easily, dip a palette knife in boiling water and use this to gently smooth the icing over the surface of the cake.

Orange torte

My mum's friend Maxine gave me this amazingly easy recipe. It uses unpeeled oranges, steamed and puréed, making the cake gorgeously moist with a taste that is unsurprisingly reminiscent of marmalade.

Serves 8–10 (v)

PREPARATION TIME
5 minutes

COOKING TIME
1¼ hours

2 oranges, cut in half and all pips removed

200g (7oz) ground almonds

200g (7oz) caster sugar

6 eggs

1 tsp baking powder

23cm (9in) diameter spring-form/loose-bottomed cake tin

* First steam the orange halves for 30 minutes, in a steamer or in a metal sieve covered with foil and set over a saucepan of simmering water.

* Meanwhile, preheat the oven to 180°C (350°F), Gas mark 4. Line the base of the tin with a disc of baking parchment and grease the sides with butter.

* Once the oranges have finished steaming, remove from the steamer or sieve and discard any remaining pips. Place the steamed oranges in a food processor with the remaining ingredients and whiz for 2 minutes or until smooth.

* Tip the mixture into the prepared tin and bake in the oven for 40–45 minutes or until a skewer inserted into the centre of the cake comes out clean. Allow to stand in the tin for 10 minutes before transferring to a wire rack to cool.

Orange and almond cake

Fresh from the oven, this rich almond cake is drenched in a sweet citrus syrup, making it fantastically moist and full of flavour. Being so moist means it will keep, covered, for up to a week. The cake is delicious on its own or with a dollop of Greek yoghurt.

Serves 6–8 (v)

PREPARATION TIME
10 minutes

COOKING TIME
1¼ hours

200g (7oz) butter, softened and diced

275g (10oz) caster sugar

Finely grated zest of 2 oranges

Finely grated zest of 1 lemon

5 eggs

350g (12oz) ground almonds

For the syrup

Juice of 2 oranges and 1 lemon

75g (3oz) caster sugar

23cm (9in) diameter spring-form/loose-bottomed cake tin

* Preheat the oven to 160°C (325°F), Gas mark 3. Line the base of the tin with a disc of baking parchment and grease the sides with butter.

* Using an electric food mixer or hand-held electric beater, cream the butter until soft. Add the sugar and lemon and orange zest and beat until the mixture is light and fluffy. Beat in the eggs, one at a time, before stirring in the ground almonds.

* Tip the mixture into the prepared tin and bake for 55–60 minutes or until a skewer inserted into the centre of the cake comes out clean. Remove from the oven and allow to cool in the tin for 10–15 minutes before transferring to a plate or cake stand.

* While the cake is cooling, make the syrup. Pour the orange and lemon juice into a saucepan, add the sugar and bring to the boil, stirring to dissolve the sugar. Boil for about 10 minutes or until the liquid has thickened to a syrupy consistency.

* Make 10–15 skewer incisions in the top of the cooled cake, then gradually pour the boiling syrup over the cake so that it absorbs the syrup evenly and becomes deliciously moist. Cut into slices to serve.

Gluten-free chocolate and orange polenta cake

This cake has no flour (hence no gluten), making it light and moist. The polenta gives it a slight crunch. I like to have a slice of this cake with tea – if I can stick to just one slice, that is …

Serves 6–8 (v)

PREPARATION TIME
20 minutes

COOKING TIME
35 minutes

200g (7oz) dark chocolate, broken into pieces, or dark chocolate drops

100g (3½oz) butter

5 eggs, separated

225g (8oz) caster sugar

75g (3oz) fine polenta

Finely grated zest of 1 orange

Icing sugar, for dusting

25cm (10in) diameter spring-form/loose-bottomed cake tin

* Preheat the oven to 160°C (325°F), Gas mark 3. Line the base of the cake tin with a disc of baking parchment and grease the sides with butter.

* Place the chocolate and butter in a heatproof bowl set over a saucepan of simmering water and allow to melt, then remove from the heat and leave to cool slightly.

* Meanwhile, place the egg yolks in a large bowl or in an electric food mixer. Add 150g (5oz) of the caster sugar and whisk in the mixer or using a hand-held electric beater for about 5 minutes or until light and fluffy. Tip into the chocolate mixture and carefully fold in.

* Wash and dry the bowl and the whisk attachments of the mixer or hand-held beater, then whisk the egg whites until they form soft peaks. Add the remaining sugar and continue to whisk meringue mixture for another 5 minutes or until stiff and white.

* Carefully fold the polenta, orange zest and the whisked egg whites into the chocolate mixture, then spoon into the prepared cake tin. Smooth over the top and bake for 25 minutes or until a skewer inserted into the centre of the cake comes out clean. Remove from the oven and allow to stand and cool slightly in the tin. Then remove the cake from the tin and allow it to cool completely on a wire rack before transferring to a serving plate and dusting with icing sugar.

Chocolate mousse

If you want a truly chocolatey and delicious dessert, then nothing beats this classic dish. Some recipes need no improving – they're classics for a reason!

Serves 8 (v)

PREPARATION TIME
10 minutes

COOKING TIME
**5 minutes,
plus chilling**

125ml (4½fl oz) double or regular cream

125g (4½oz) dark chocolate, finely chopped, or dark chocolate drops

1 tbsp brandy (optional)

2 eggs, separated

To decorate

Raspberries (optional)

Icing sugar (optional)

4–6 little bowls, glasses or cups

* Pour the cream into a saucepan and bring to the boil, then remove from the heat, add the chocolate and stir just until it melts. Add the brandy (if using) and whisk in the egg yolks.

* In a spotlessly clean bowl, whisk the egg whites until just forming stiff peaks. Spoon a small amount of whisked egg whites into the chocolate and cream mixture, then carefully fold in the rest of the egg whites, just until combined.

* Spoon into the bowls, glasses or cups and chill in the fridge for 1–2 hours or until set. Decorate with raspberries (if using) and a hint of icing sugar.

Oreo chocolate fudge sundae

Ice cream with chocolate sauce is a combination made in heaven and the chunks of Oreo biscuit just add to the divine wickedness of it all! This great chocolate fudge sauce recipe is one I was kindly given by the indefatigable American cook, Charita Jones. It makes quite a lot, but, in a household of chocoholics, that is never a problem! Stored in a jar in the fridge, it will keep for months – simply reheat to serve.

Serves 1 (v)

Charita's chocolate fudge sauce: makes 1 litre (1¾ pints) (v)

PREPARATION TIME
10 minutes

COOKING TIME
5 minutes

For Charita's chocolate fudge sauce

350g (12oz) caster sugar

100g (3½oz) soft light or dark brown sugar

85g (3oz) cocoa powder

25g (1oz) plain flour

Pinch of salt

1 x 400ml tin of evaporated milk

50g (2oz) butter

2 tsp vanilla extract

For each sundae

2 Oreo biscuits, broken into chunks

2 scoops of coffee, vanilla or even banana ice cream

One sundae glass or bowl per person

* To make the chocolate fudge sauce, place all the ingredients apart from the vanilla extract in a saucepan with 225ml (8fl oz) water and bring to the boil, stirring constantly. Boil for about 5 minutes or until slightly thickened, using a whisk at first to break up any lumps of flour. Remove from the heat and stir in the vanilla extract.

* To make each sundae, place half the biscuit pieces in the bottom of the glass or bowl, add a scoop of ice cream, then add most of the remaining biscuit pieces, followed by the remaining scoop of ice cream. Pour over the hot chocolate fudge sauce and crumble over the rest of the biscuit pieces.

Toffee peanut sundae

Sundaes are a huge favourite of my children's, but anyone with a sweet tooth is susceptible to an ice cream sundae. It's great to have a few sauces and ingredients on hand so people can get creative. The toffee sauce used in this recipe takes minutes to make and is so useful to have for pouring over ice cream, meringues or even baked fruit, such as peaches, pears or bananas. Once made, it keeps for months, so I always have a jar of it nestled somewhere in the back of the fridge. Simply reheat to serve.

Serves 1 (v)

Toffee sauce: enough for 4 sundaes (v)

PREPARATION TIME
10 minutes

COOKING TIME
5 minutes

For the toffee sauce

100ml (3½fl oz) golden syrup

50g (2oz) soft light brown sugar

50g (2oz) caster sugar

½ tsp vanilla extract

100ml (3½fl oz) double or regular cream

For each sundae

2 scoops of chocolate or vanilla ice cream

2 tbsp salted peanuts

One sundae glass or bowl per person

* To make the toffee sauce, place all the ingredients in a saucepan and bring to the boil, stirring constantly to help dissolve the sugar. Boil for 5 minutes or until the sauce has thickened, then remove from the heat.

* To make each sundae, place one scoop of ice cream in the bottom of the glass or bowl, add half the peanuts, then add another scoop of ice cream, followed by the rest of the peanuts, and finally drizzle with the hot toffee sauce.

Chocolate marshmallow biscuit cake

My children would survive solely on this given half a chance. You can use whatever biscuits or chocolate bars you like, although ginger biscuits add a great spicy crunch.

Makes about 16 bars (v)

PREPARATION TIME
10 minutes, plus chilling

COOKING TIME
10 minutes

450g (1lb) milk chocolate, broken into pieces, or milk chocolate drops

150g (5oz) ginger nut biscuits, broken into 1cm (½in) chunks

100g (3½oz) mini marshmallows

2 x 60g Snickers bars, cut into 1cm (½in) cubes

2 x 40g Crunchie bars, cut into 1cm (½in) cubes

20cm (8in) square cake tin

* Line the base and sides of the tin with baking parchment.

* Place the chocolate in a heatproof bowl set over a saucepan of hot water. Bring the water to the boil, then take the pan off the heat and allow the chocolate to melt slowly. Once the chocolate has melted, remove the bowl from the saucepan and allow the chocolate to cool to just above room temperature. (If it's too hot, the marshmallows will melt.)

* Stir in the remaining ingredients and press into the prepared tin. Place in the fridge to chill for 1–2 hours or until set, then cut into fingers or squares to serve.

Fruit sundae with strawberry coulis

Strawberry coulis is such a useful sauce for pouring over ice cream, yoghurt or fromage frais. Use straightaway or store in the fridge, in a covered bowl or jar with a lid, for up to a week. It can also be frozen for up to one month.

Serves 1 (v)

Strawberry coulis: enough for 4 sundaes (v)

PREPARATION TIME
10 minutes

For the strawberry coulis

150g (5oz) fresh strawberries, hulled and sliced, or frozen strawberries, defrosted

2 tsp caster sugar

Juice of ½ lemon

For each sundae

6–8 slices tinned peaches or nectarines

2–3 strawberries, sliced

3 scoops of ice cream, such as vanilla or strawberry

One sundae glass or bowl per sundae

* To make the strawberry coulis, place everything in a food processor and whiz for 1–2 minutes or until smooth. (If using frozen and defrosted strawberries, you can simply mash these with a fork, if you prefer.) Taste to see if you need to add any more sugar or lemon juice – the blander the strawberries, the more help they'll need.

* Push the purée through a fine sieve, discarding any pulp, and use straightaway or keep chilled in the fridge for future use.

* To make each sundae, place half the peaches or nectarines and strawberry slices in the bottom of the glass or bowl, add a scoop of ice cream and drizzle with half the coulis, then add the remaining fruit, followed by another scoop of ice cream, and drizzle with the rest of the coulis.

Variation

Raspberry coulis: Make as above but substitute the strawberries with the same quantity of fresh or frozen (and defrosted) raspberries.

Raspberry coconut pudding

This incredibly easy recipe has become a new family favourite!
I adore the combination of ingredients – the moist coconutty
sponge sits over a layer of sweet and sticky raspberry jam.
It's lovely on its own, though it's also excellent with custard.

Serves 6–8 (v)

PREPARATION TIME
10 minutes

COOKING TIME
40–50 minutes

4 tbsp raspberry jam

250g (9oz) plain flour

3 tsp baking powder

350g (12oz) caster sugar

100g (3½oz) desiccated
coconut

3 eggs, beaten

350ml (12fl oz) milk

1 tsp vanilla extract

150g (5oz) butter, melted

2 litre (3½ pint) pie dish

* Preheat the oven to 180°C (350°F), Gas mark 4.

* Spread the jam over the base of the pie dish. Sift the
flour and baking powder into a bowl, add the rest of the
ingredients and whisk them by hand just long enough to
mix them together.

* Pour the coconut mixture into the pie dish and bake
for 40–50 minutes or until the top is golden brown and
the centre has a light spring when pressed with your
finger. Remove from the oven and allow to cool slightly
before serving.

Coconut and cardamom pannacotta

A classic pannacotta contains only cream, but I've added coconut milk and cardamom for a tropical twist. It is delicious served with slices of juicy ripe mango.

Serves 4–6

PREPARATION TIME
10 minutes

COOKING TIME
5 minutes,
plus chilling

12 green cardamom pods

150ml (5fl oz) single, double or regular cream

75g (3oz) caster sugar

2 leaves of gelatine or 2 tsp powdered gelatine

1 x 400ml tin of coconut milk

1 mango, peeled and cut into slices, to decorate

4–6 small cups or glasses

* Place the cardamom pods on a chopping board, lay the flat side of a large knife over the top and press down to lightly crush. Remove the seeds (discarding the pods) and crush to a powder with a pestle and mortar or place in a plastic bag and use a rolling pin to crush them.

* Place the crushed seeds in a saucepan and add the cream and sugar. Bring to the boil, stirring constantly to dissolve the sugar. When the sugar has dissolved, remove from the heat and leave to infuse.

* If using powdered gelatine, place this in a bowl with 2 tablespoons of water and leave in the fridge for 3–4 minutes or until the mixture becomes sponge-like in consistency. If using leaf gelatine, place the leaves in a bowl, adding just enough cold water to cover, and set aside for 5 minutes or until the gelatine has become very soft.

* Empty the tin of coconut milk into a large bowl, whisking it to get rid of any lumps. Place the cream mixture back on a medium heat just to heat through, then remove from the hob. If using powdered gelatine, mix the spongey mixture in with the coconut milk. If using leaf gelatine, remove from the water, allowing any excess to drip off, then stir into the coconut milk. Mix together thoroughly, then pour the coconut milk and gelatine through a sieve onto the cream mixture and stir to mix.

* Divide between the cups or glasses and chill in the fridge for about 3 hours or until just set. Serve topped with some mango slices.

Vanilla buttercream squares

The sponge in this tray bake is light and delightfully delicate, though the truth is this recipe is all about the rich and sweet icing. Is there anything more invitingly indulgent than buttercream?

Makes 16 squares (v)

PREPARATION TIME
5–10 minutes

COOKING TIME
40 minutes

200g (7oz) butter, softened and diced

200g (7oz) caster sugar

3 eggs

325g (11½oz) plain flour, sifted

3 tsp baking powder

2 tsp vanilla extract

150ml (5fl oz) milk

For the vanilla buttercream icing

150g (5oz) butter, softened and diced

200g (7oz) icing sugar, sifted

2 tsp vanilla extract

2 tbsp milk

20cm (8in) square cake tin

* Preheat the oven to 180°C (350°F), Gas mark 4. Line the base of the tin with baking parchment and grease the sides with butter.

* Place all the ingredients for the sponge in a food processor and whiz for 1 minute or just until combined. Alternatively, cream the butter until soft using a hand-held electric beater, then beat in the sugar, whisk in the eggs one at a time and fold in the remaining ingredients.

* Tip the mixture into the prepared tin, smooth over the top and bake in the oven for 40 minutes or until a skewer inserted into the centre of the cake comes out clean. Remove from the oven and allow the cake to stand for 10 minutes in the tin before transferring to a wire rack to cool completely.

* While the cake is cooling, make the icing. Place all the ingredients in the food processor, having cleaned the bowl and mixer blade, and whiz until light and fluffy. Alternatively, cream the butter until soft using the electric beater, then beat in the remaining ingredients.

* Place the cake on a plate and spread the icing over the top using a palette knife, then cut into squares and serve.

Ginger squares with lime frosting

The lime frosting gives these spicy sponge squares real zing. Because they are so wonderfully moist they will keep, covered, for up to a week.

Makes 30 squares (v)

PREPARATION TIME
5–10 minutes

COOKING TIME
20–25 minutes

250g (9oz) butter, softened and diced

150g (5oz) caster sugar

100ml (3½fl oz) black treacle

3 eggs

250g (9oz) plain flour, sifted

2 tsp baking powder

3 tsp ground ginger

1 tsp ground cinnamon

2 tbsp milk

For the lime frosting

225g (8oz) cream cheese

75g (3oz) caster sugar

Finely grated zest and juice of 1 lime

20 x 30cm (8 x 12in) Swiss roll tin

* Preheat the oven to 180°C (350°F), Gas mark 4. Line the base of the Swiss roll tin with baking parchment and grease the sides with butter.

* Place all the ingredients for the sponge in a food processor and whiz for 1 minute or just until combined. Alternatively, cream the butter until soft using a hand-held electric beater, then beat in the sugar and treacle, whisk in the eggs one at a time and fold in the remaining ingredients.

* Tip the mixture into the prepared tin, smooth over the top and bake for 20–25 minutes or until lightly browned and springy to the touch. Carefully tip out onto a wire rack, peel away the baking parchment and allow to cool.

* While the sponge is cooling, make the lime frosting. Place all the ingredients in the food processor, having first cleaned the bowl and mixer blade, and whiz until light and fuffy. Alternatively, cream all the ingredients together using the electric beater. Spread over the sponge and cut into squares to serve.

Fast and Fabulous

These recipes speak for themselves – they're incredibly flavourful and delicious, but can all be made in under a half hour. This is the kind of food that's perfect for a midweek supper when you've just come home from work but still want something quite special. Even though these are done in a flash, they are impressive enough to serve to even the most discerning guest!

Parsnip soup with porcini oil

This simple parsnip soup is given a drizzling of luxury with some easy-to-make porcini oil. Porcini mushrooms are available in delis, specialist food shops and some supermarkets.

Serves 4 (v)

PREPARATION TIME
10 minutes

COOKING TIME
20 minutes

50g (2oz) butter

1 small onion, peeled and roughly chopped

350g (12oz) parsnips, peeled and roughly chopped

550ml (19fl oz) vegetable (or chicken) stock

150ml (5fl oz) single or regular cream, or 75ml (3fl oz) milk and 75ml (3fl oz) cream

Salt and freshly ground black pepper

For the porcini oil

100ml (3½fl oz) olive oil

15g (½oz) dried porcini mushrooms

* To make the porcini oil, pour the olive oil into a small saucepan on a medium–low heat, add the mushrooms and cook very gently for 6–8 minutes, then remove from the hob, strain the mushrooms (reserving the infused oil) and set aside.

* While the mushrooms are cooking, make the soup. Melt the butter in a large saucepan on a low heat, add the onion and parsnips, cover with a butter wrapper or piece of greaseproof paper and cook, stirring occasionally, for 6–8 minutes or until they are softened but not browned.

* Pour in the stock, then bring to the boil, reduce the heat and simmer for a further 10 minutes or until the parsnips have completely softened. Using a blender or hand-held blender, whiz the parsnips until smooth, then return to the heat, stir in the cream or milk and cream and season to taste with salt and pepper.

* To serve, ladle the soup into bowls and drizzle with about a teaspoon of the porcini oil (but not the mushrooms themselves) and top with a grinding of black pepper.

Speedy chicken noodle soup

This is a supremely easy soup to put together. The Thai flavours are wonderfully refreshing, while the rice noodles and slivers of cooked chicken make it quite substantial too.

Serves 4

PREPARATION TIME
7 minutes

COOKING TIME
5 minutes

100g (3½oz) medium rice noodles

800ml (1 pint 9fl oz) chicken stock

2 cloves of garlic, peeled and crushed or finely grated

4 x 2–3mm (⅝in) thick slices of unpeeled root ginger

300g (11oz) chicken breast or thigh meat, very thinly sliced

2–3 tbsp fish sauce (nam pla)

Juice of 1 lime or ½ lemon

4 spring onions, trimmed and sliced at an angle

4 tbsp roughly chopped coriander

* Place the rice noodles in a bowl, cover with boiling water and allow to soak for 4–5 minutes, or according to the instructions on the packet, until softened.

* While they are soaking, place the stock in a saucepan with the garlic and ginger. Bring to the boil, then add the chicken and cook for 2 minutes until the chicken is opaque. Add the fish sauce and lime juice to taste, then add in the spring onions and coriander.

* Drain the noodles and divide between four warmed bowls, top with the soup and serve.

Variation

Speedy prawn noodle soup: Make as above, substituting the chicken with the same weight of finely sliced, raw, peeled tiger prawns.

Five-minute pea soup

I challenge anyone to make a fresh soup any faster than this. It is perfect as an emergency starter or quick lunch. You don't even need to defrost the peas!

Serves 4 (v)

PREPARATION TIME
2 minutes

COOKING TIME
3 minutes

500ml (18fl oz) vegetable (or chicken) stock

200g (7oz) frozen peas

2 cloves of garlic, peeled and finely grated

2 spring onions, trimmed and sliced

Salt and freshly ground black pepper

100ml (3½fl oz) single or regular cream

3 tsp chopped tarragon

* Put the stock, frozen peas, garlic and the spring onions into a large saucepan on a high heat, season with salt and pepper and bring to the boil.

* Add the cream and tarragon and liquidise in a blender or using a hand-held blender. Pour the soup into the saucepan and heat through on the hob. Season with salt and pepper to taste and serve with crusty bread.

Chickpea and aubergine salad

I love the contrasting textures and flavours in this salad. Easy to assemble it is delicious by itself, though it also goes well with grilled lamb chops or the Rack of Lamb on page 186.

Rack of Lamb on page 186.

Serves 4–6 (v)

PREPARATION TIME
10 minutes

COOKING TIME
20 minutes

4 red onions, peeled and cut through the root into 8 wedges

2 large or 4 medium aubergines, cut into 1–2cm (½–¾in) cubes

150ml (5fl oz) olive oil

Salt and freshly ground black pepper

2 x 400g tins of chickpeas, drained and rinsed

4 handfuls of rocket leaves

For the dressing

400ml (14fl oz) natural yoghurt

1 tsp smoked paprika

4 tbsp chopped mint

* Preheat the oven to 220°C (425°F), Gas mark 7.

* Place the onion wedges in a bowl with the aubergine pieces, pour over the olive oil, season with salt and pepper and stir together to combine. Spread out on a baking tray and roast in the oven for 18–20 minutes or until the vegetables are softened and lightly browned.

* Meanwhile, place the chickpeas in a bowl and season with salt and pepper, then make the dressing by mixing the yoghurt with the paprika and mint in another bowl.

* To serve, mix together the roasted onion and aubergine with the chickpeas, then place in one large serving dish or divide between individual plates, drizzle with the yoghurt dressing and scatter the rocket leaves on top.

Fattoush

Fattoush is a Middle Eastern salad that includes bread and a mixture of different vegetables. Sumac – a powdered red spice made from berries of the sumac tree – is traditionally used to give fattoush its characteristic sour taste. You can get hold of it in specialist food shops and some big supermarkets. Though it is optional in this recipe, I urge you to seek some out as it is a unique and worthwhile Middle Eastern flavouring.

Serves 4

PREPARATION TIME
10 minutes

COOKING TIME
8–10 minutes

2 round pitta breads or 1 large oval pitta, cut into bite-sized chunks

5 tbsp olive oil

Salt and freshly ground black pepper

½ cucumber, cut into 2cm (¾in) chunks

3 tomatoes, cut into 2cm (¾in) chunks

½ red onion, peeled and thinly sliced

1 small red pepper, deseeded and cut into 2cm (¾in) chunks

2 tbsp chopped coriander

2 tsp sumac (optional)

Finely grated zest and juice of ½ lemon

1 clove of garlic, peeled and crushed

1 tsp red wine vinegar

Pinch of granulated or caster sugar

* Preheat the oven to 180°C (350°F), Gas mark 4.

* Toss the pitta bread wedges or chunks in 2 tablespoons of the olive oil and season with salt and pepper. Spread out on a baking sheet and roast in the oven for 8–10 minutes or until golden.

* Place the remaining ingredients in a bowl, add the roasted pitta pieces, then mix everything together, seasoning to taste with salt and pepper and a pinch of sugar.

Spicy prawns with feta and watermelon

Watermelon and feta is a tried and tested combination. Crunchy watermelon beautifully complements the soft, salty hit of feta.

24–32 raw, peeled tiger prawns

4 lime wedges, to serve

For the marinade

4 cloves of garlic, peeled and crushed or finely grated

2 tsp peeled and finely chopped root ginger

1 tsp ground cumin

1 tsp ground coriander

1 tsp ground fennel

4 tbsp sesame oil

2 tsp Tabasco sauce

2 tsp soft light brown sugar

For the watermelon and feta salad

300g (11oz) (prepared weight) watermelon, peeled and cut into 1cm (½in) cubes

16 black olives, pitted and roughly chopped (optional)

Juice of 1 lime

1 tbsp chopped basil

1 tbsp chopped mint

110g (4oz) feta cheese, crumbled

4–8 metal or wooden skewers, depending on size, which will also depend on the size of your frying pan

Serves 4

PREPARATION TIME
5 minutes, plus marinating

COOKING TIME
10 minutes

* If using wooden skewers, place the skewers in a bowl, cover with boiling water and leave to soak to prevent them burning during cooking.

* In a separate bowl, mix all the ingredients for the marinade. Add the prawns, cover with cling film or a plate and set aside for at least 15 minutes.

* Meanwhile, place the ingredients for the salad in a bowl and mix together.

* Thread 6–8 prawns on each skewer, taking care to arrange the prawns side on and facing the same way so that each skewer is as flat as possible and the prawns cook evenly.

* Place a heavy-based frying pan or griddle pan on a high heat and, when hot, add the skewers, cooking them for 3–4 minutes on each side or until they are deliciously golden on the outside and opaque all the way through.

* To serve, spoon the salad on to each plate and arrange a prawn skewer or two on top and add lime wedges.

Roasted vegetable couscous

Roasting vegetables concentrates their flavour as the water in them evaporates and the sugars caramelise. This recipe does require a bit of preparing, but with the main ingredients being cooked at the same time, it doesn't take long overall, and what you get in return is a dish full of warm spicy flavours and interesting textures.

Serves 4

PREPARATION TIME
10 minutes

COOKING TIME
20 minutes

2 tsp cumin seeds

2 tsp coriander seeds

2 tsp fennel seeds

1 red pepper, deseeded and cut into 1cm (½in) dice

1 courgette (about 20cm/8in long), cut into 1cm (½in) dice

1 aubergine, cut into 1cm (½in) dice

100ml (4fl oz) olive oil

Salt and freshly ground black pepper

2 red onions, peeled and thinly sliced

200g (7oz) feta cheese, cut into 1cm (½in) cubes

250g (9oz) couscous

250ml (9fl oz) hot vegetable (or chicken) stock

2 tbsp chopped parsley

* Preheat the oven to 230°C (450°F), Gas mark 8.

* Toast and grind the cumin, coriander and fennel seeds. First place them in a small frying pan on a high heat and cook, tossing frequently, for about 1 minute or until they are browned (taking care not to let them burn). Grind them into a powder with a pestle and mortar or place the seeds in a plastic bag and use a rolling pin to crush them, then set aside.

* Place the red pepper, courgette and aubergine pieces in a bowl, then pour over 50ml (2fl oz) of the olive oil and mix well together, seasoning generously with salt and pepper. Spread out on a baking tray and roast in the oven for 20 minutes, tossing occasionally, until the vegetables are soft and lightly browned.

* Meanwhile, pour 25ml (1fl oz) of the olive oil into a frying pan on a medium–high heat, add the sliced onions, season with salt and pepper and fry, stirring occasionally, for 15–20 minutes or until the onions are golden and completely soft.

* Meanwhile, place the feta in a bowl, along with the remaining olive oil and the spices, and set aside.

* Finally, 5 minutes before the vegetables and onions are ready, mix together the couscous with the hot stock in a large bowl and allow to stand for 5 minutes or until the liquid has been absorbed. Use a fork to fluff up the grains of couscous.

* Add the roasted vegetables and parsley to the couscous and gently mix everything together. Check the seasoning, then divide between bowls to serve.

Zac's omelette wraps

My husband Isaac makes these quick, thin omelettes as a wrap for a variety of fillings (for my favourites, see the next page). They are great hot and make a refreshing change to tortilla wraps. You can make a few in advance and serve them cold, too – so versatile.

Makes 1 (v)

PREPARATION TIME
10 minutes, including fillings

COOKING TIME
5 minutes

For each wrap

2 eggs

1 tbsp milk

Salt and freshly ground black pepper

15g (½oz) butter

Filling of choice (see next page)

* Whisk the eggs together with the milk and season with salt and pepper.

* Melt the butter in a large frying pan on a high heat and, when foaming, pour in the egg mixture, but without stirring as you would with a standard omelette.

* Fry for 2 minutes or until golden underneath, then flip the omelette over and cook on the other side for a further 2 minutes. Slide the omelette out onto a plate, add your filling of choice (see next page) and roll up the omelette wrap to serve.

Continued on the next page...

Avocado salsa filling (v)

3 tsp crème fraîche

¼ avocado, sliced or cubed

½ tomato, sliced or cubed

1 spring onion, trimmed and chopped

2 tsp chopped coriander

Salt and freshly ground black pepper

Squeeze of lime juice

* Spread the crème fraîche in a single layer on the finished omelette, then arrange the avocado, tomato, spring onion and chopped coriander down the centre of the wrap. Season with salt and pepper and a squeeze of lime, then roll up the omelette and serve.

Cheese and ham filling

50g (2oz) cheese, such as Gruyère, grated

2 slices cooked ham (about 40g/1½oz), chopped

Few slices of tomato

1 spring onion, trimmed and sliced

3–4 basil leaves, torn

Salt and freshly ground black pepper

* For this wrap, don't flip the omelette over. Instead, add the cheese to the omelette then place under a hot grill for 2–3 minutes.
* Slide onto a plate then arrange the remaining ingredients down the centre of the wrap before seasoning with a little salt and pepper and rolling up to serve.

Smoked salmon and creme fresh filling

3 tsp crème fraîche

50g (2oz) smoked salmon, sliced

½ tbsp capers (about 8–10), drained and rinsed

½ tbsp chopped chives

Salt and freshly ground black pepper

Squeeze of lemon juice

* Spread the crème fraîche in a single layer on the finished omelette, then arrange the smoked salmon, capers and chives down the centre of the wrap. Season with salt and pepper and a squeeze of lemon, then roll up the omelette and serve.

Mushroom and Gruyère tart

This is a truly gorgeous mixture of flavour and texture – crisp buttery pastry topped with soft garlicky mushrooms and melted golden Gruyère. For a slightly different take on this tart, you can substitute standard Gruyère with the delicious Irish farmhouse version, Glebe Brethan.

Serves 4 (v)

PREPARATION TIME
5 minutes

COOKING TIME
30–35 minutes

25g (1oz) butter

300g (11oz) flat mushrooms, cut into 5mm (¼in) thick slices

3 cloves of garlic, peeled and finely chopped

1 tbsp chopped thyme leaves

Salt and freshly ground black pepper

500g (1lb 2oz) ready-rolled puff pastry (or roll out a block of puff pastry to a thickness of about 4mm/⅛in)

75g (3oz) grated Gruyère cheese

* Preheat the oven to 220°C (425°F), Gas mark 7.

* Melt the butter in a large frying pan on a high heat and, when foaming, add the mushrooms, garlic and half the thyme leaves. Season with salt and pepper and cook, stirring occasionally, for about 5 minutes or until the mushrooms have darkened and are just tender, then remove from the heat.

* Trim the pastry into a 25–30cm (10–12in) rectangle, then transfer to a baking sheet. Sprinkle over the cheese, leaving a border of about 1cm (½in) all the way round, then spoon the mushrooms on top, spreading them out in a single layer.

* Place in the oven and bake for 20–25 minutes or until the pastry is golden and the mushrooms are bubbling hot. Remove from the oven, sprinkle over the remaining thyme leaves and serve.

Tomato and goat's cheese tart

The sweetness of fresh tomatoes balances the sharp creaminess of soft goat's cheese. Drizzled with a little pesto, this super easy tart makes a lovely summer starter or light lunch.

Serves 6–8

PREPARATION TIME
10 minutes

COOKING TIME
20–25 minutes

400g (14oz) tomatoes, sliced

1 red onion, peeled and cut through the root into 8 wedges

2 tbsp olive oil

Salt and freshly ground black pepper

Good pinch of granulated or caster sugar

500g (1lb 5oz) ready-rolled puff pastry (or roll out a block of puff pastry to a thickness of about 4mm/⅛in)

75g (3oz) soft goat's cheese

2 tbsp pesto

* Preheat the oven to 220°C (425°F), Gas mark 7.

* Place the tomato slices and onion wedges in a bowl, then add the olive oil, gently stir together and season with salt and pepper and the sugar. Trim the pastry into a 25–30cm (10–12in) rectangle and transfer to a baking sheet.

* Arrange the tomato and onion on the pastry in rows, leaving a 1cm (½in) border all the way round then dot spoonfuls of the goat's cheese at regular intervals on top of the tomatoes and onion.

* Bake for 20–25 minutes or until the pastry is golden and the tomatoes cooked through and bubbling hot. Remove from the oven and drizzle with the pesto, then serve immediately.

Piadine

A type of thin Italian flatbread, piadine are extremely quick to prepare and cook. I've provided a few suggestions for some Italian-style toppings on the next page, but you can top them with anything that takes your fancy.

Makes 4 piadine (v)

PREPARATION TIME
15 minutes, including fillings

COOKING TIME
25–30 minutes

250g (9oz) plain flour, plus extra for dusting

½ tsp salt

½ tsp baking powder

¼ tsp baking soda

50g (2oz) butter, softened and diced

50ml (2fl oz) milk

50ml (2fl oz) warm water

Topping of choice (see next page)

Heavy-based frying pan or griddle pan at least 20cm (8in) in diameter

* Sift the flour into a bowl with the salt, baking powder and baking soda. Rub in the butter with your fingertips until the mixture resembles coarse breadcrumbs, then mix the milk with the warm water and pour into the dry ingredients, kneading the dough to bring it together.

* Once it comes together, place the ball of dough on a work surface and cover with the upturned bowl. Allow to rest for at least 5 minutes while you prepare your chosen topping (see next page).

* Divide the dough into 4 and, on a work surface lightly dusted with flour, roll each ball of dough into a round about 20cm (8in) in diameter and 3–4mm (⅛in) thick.

* Place the frying pan or griddle pan (if you would like deep golden score marks on the cooked piadine) on a medium–high heat and allow to get hot. (There's no need to grease the pan.) Place one of the piadine in the hot pan and cook for 3–4 minutes on each side or until golden brown spots appear (or lines, if using a griddle pan). Repeat with the remaining piadine.

* Serve straightaway or keep wrapped up in a clean tea towel so they remain soft. Top each piadine with your chosen topping (see next page), then cut into wedges or fold in half to serve.

Continued on the next page...

Piadine (cont.)

Kale and prosciutto topping

2 tbsp olive oil

150g (5oz) (prepared weight) kale leaves, stalks and centre ribs removed and leaves shredded

1 clove of garlic, peeled and very thinly sliced

Salt and freshly ground black pepper

8 slices of prosciutto

4 tbsp ricotta or mascarpone

Mushroom and pesto topping

15g (½oz) butter

300g (11oz) flat or button mushrooms, thinly sliced

Salt and freshly ground black pepper

100ml (3½fl oz) single or regular cream

4 tsp pesto

25g (1oz) Parmesan cheese, grated

Smoked salmon and cream cheese topping

100g (3½oz) smoked salmon, thinly sliced

4 tbsp cream cheese

¼ red onion, peeled and very thinly sliced

1 tbsp capers, drained and rinsed

Quesadillas

Biting into a cheesy quesadilla is one of the great pleasures of Mexican food and they take only minutes to make. They are traditionally filled with chicken or pork but I've given you a few simpler variations. Serve as a starter, light lunch or snack.

Makes 1

PREPARATION TIME
**10 minutes,
including fillings**

COOKING TIME
10 minutes

For each quesadilla

1 wheat flour tortilla

Filling of choice (see below)

Gruyère and mango filling (v)

75g (3oz) Gruyère cheese, grated

1 tbsp chopped coriander

3 tbsp peeled and chopped mango

1 spring onion, trimmed and sliced

Pinch of finely chopped red chilli
(optional)

Salami and mozzarella filling

75g (3oz) mozzarella, grated

1 tsp pesto

1 tsp olive oil

3 slices of salami, cut into pieces

Tomato and goat's cheese filling (v)

50g (2oz) mozzarella, grated

25g (1oz) soft goat's cheese, crumbled

6 black or green olives, pitted and chopped

2 tsp chopped sun-dried tomatoes

* Mix all the ingredients of the filling of your choice together in a bowl.

* Place a frying pan (large enough to fit one tortilla) on a medium heat. While it is heating, fold the tortilla in half, then unfold it again so that you can easily see the two halves. Place in the hot, dry pan and arrange your filling on one half of the tortilla, forming a half-moon shape and spreading it to within 2cm (¾in) of the edges.

* Fold over the other half of the tortilla, press down with the flat of your hand or a spatula and cook for 3–4 minutes or until golden brown underneath, then press down on it again to help it stick together.

* Flip the quesadilla over and cook on the other side for another 3–4 minutes. By the time it's turned golden brown underneath, the cheese should all be melted in the centre. Lift an edge of the tortilla to check. If it's not fully melted, then turn the heat down to low and cook for another minute or two until it is. Cut into wedges and serve immediately.

Fusilli with courgettes and lemon

Courgettes demand lemons: their juice and zest provide the accompaniment that lets a courgette sing. Best served outside on a warm summer's day.

Serves 4

PREPARATION TIME
10 minutes

COOKING TIME
10–12 minutes

Salt and freshly ground black pepper

350g (12oz) dried fusilli or other pasta, such as farfalle or conchiglie

2 tbsp olive oil

1 large or 2 medium courgettes (about 450g/1lb in total), halved lengthways and cut at an angle into 3mm (⅛in) thick slices

125g (4½oz) mascarpone

1 tsp finely grated lemon zest

1 tbsp lemon juice, plus extra to taste

25g (1oz) Parmesan cheese, grated, to serve

* Fill a large saucepan with water, add 1 teaspoon of salt and bring to the boil, then add the fusilli and cook for 10–12 minutes, or according to the instructions on the packet, until al dente.

* While the pasta is cooking, pour the olive oil into a frying pan on a high heat. When the oil is hot, add the courgettes, season with salt and pepper and sauté, tossing regularly, for 3 minutes or until just softened and a little golden. Remove from the heat and set aside.

* Drain the pasta, retaining about 50ml (2fl oz) of the cooking liquid, then stir in the reserved liquid with the mascarpone, lemon zest and juice and the fried courgettes. Season with salt, pepper and extra lemon juice to taste and serve with some Parmesan cheese grated over the top.

Spiced prawns, tomatoes and chickpeas

I like the way the chickpeas in this dish add both texture and bulk, helping the prawns go a little further. The sweetness of the prawns really complements the smokiness of the paprika and the gentle kick of the chilli.

Serves 4–6

PREPARATION TIME
10 minutes

COOKING TIME
25 minutes

3 tbsp olive oil

1 onion, peeled and sliced

2 cloves of garlic, peeled and crushed or finely grated

½ tsp smoked paprika

¼–½ red chilli, deseeded and finely chopped

Salt and freshly ground black pepper

1 x 400g tin of chopped tomatoes

½ tsp caster sugar

1 x 400g tin of chickpeas, drained and rinsed

450g (1lb) raw, peeled tiger prawns

Juice of 1 lime or ½ lemon

2 tbsp chopped coriander

* Pour the olive oil into a saucepan on a high heat and, when hot, tip in the onion, garlic, paprika and chilli and season with salt and pepper. Sauté for 5–6 minutes, stirring frequently, until the onion is soft and turning golden around the edges.

* Add the tomatoes, sugar, chickpeas and 100ml (3½ fl oz) water, bring to the boil, then reduce the heat to low and simmer for 10 minutes.

* Add the prawns to the pan and simmer for 3–5 minutes or until opaque, then stir in the lime or lemon juice and most of the coriander, seasoning with salt and pepper to taste. Serve with boiled rice (see page 332) and the rest of the coriander sprinkled over the top.

Quick prawn korma

One of the benefits of prawns is how quickly they cook. Here they are flavoured with a combination of spices, coconut and a little yoghurt in a delicious korma-like sauce. You can also use pre-cooked prawns – just add them with the spices.

Serves 4

PREPARATION TIME
10 minutes

COOKING TIME
20 minutes

4 green cardamom pods

1 tsp fennel seeds

4 cloves

3 tbsp sunflower oil

2 onions, peeled and finely chopped

4 cloves of garlic, peeled and finely chopped

1 tsp peeled and finely grated root ginger

Salt and freshly ground black pepper

1 tsp ground cinnamon

400g (14oz) raw, peeled tiger prawns

4 tbsp natural yoghurt

4 tbsp desiccated coconut

* To remove the seeds from the cardamom pods, place the pods on a chopping board, lay the flat side of a large knife over the top and press down to lightly crush. Remove the seeds (discarding the pods) and add to the fennel seeds and cloves, then crush to a powder with a pestle and mortar or place in a plastic bag and use a rolling pin to crush them.

* Next, pour the sunflower oil into a large frying pan on a medium–low heat and, when hot, add the onions, garlic and ginger and season with salt and pepper. Cook for about 10 minutes, stirring frequently, until the onion is completely soft and lightly browned.

* Add the freshly ground spices and the cinnamon, then, after 30 seconds, increase the heat to medium and tip in the prawns. Cook for 2–3 minutes until opaque and firm, then stir in the yoghurt 1 tablespoon at a time so that it doesn't curdle.

* Stir in 200ml (7fl oz) water, followed by the coconut, then bring to a simmer and allow to bubble for 2 minutes. Taste for seasoning then serve with boiled rice (see page 332).

Battered prawn stir-fry

Frying prawns in batter does take a little extra effort, but it gives them a gorgeous crunch while keeping the flesh moist. The mangetout or green beans add colour and texture, but you can use sliced runner beans instead.

Serves 2–3

PREPARATION TIME
10 minutes

COOKING TIME
15 minutes

350ml (12fl oz) sunflower oil

100g (3½oz) cornflour

1 egg, beaten

2 tbsp sesame seeds

12 raw, peeled tiger prawns

3 cloves of garlic, peeled and crushed or finely grated

2 tsp peeled and grated root ginger

3 spring onions, trimmed and sliced at an angle

½ red chilli, deseeded and finely chopped

150g (5oz) mangetout or green beans, trimmed

2 tbsp soy sauce

2 tsp sesame oil

* Pour the sunflower oil into a wok or large, deep frying pan on a high heat and allow to get hot. The oil is ready when a small cube of bread dropped into it turns golden brown after 30 seconds.

* While the oil heats up, tip the cornflour into a bowl, together with the beaten egg, sesame seeds and 2 tablespoons of water. Stir in the prawns, then add half of the prawns to the hot oil. Cook for 2–3 minutes or until lightly golden, then lift from the wok or pan with a slotted spoon, drain on kitchen paper and repeat with the remaining prawns.

* Drain the oil from the wok or pan (see tip, below) retaining about 2 tablespoons in the wok.

* Return the wok or pan to the heat, set to high and add the garlic, ginger, spring onions and chilli. Stir-fry for 1 minute, then add the mangetout or green beans. Cook for a further minute, then stir in the fried prawns and cook for another 2 minutes.

* Pour in the soy sauce and sesame oil, stir-fry for a further 30 seconds, then serve immediately with boiled rice (see page 332) or noodles.

Rachel's tip

When you are draining the oil from the wok or pan, pour it into a heatproof dish and allow it to cool down before storing it for future use. You can reuse the oil up to 3 more times.

Thai mussels

One of the things I love about mussels is their chameleon-like quality. When teamed with white wine, garlic and parsley, they transport you immediately to a Paris bistro. Cooked Thai-style, as in this recipe, they take me much further afield – to a hot summer's evening in Southeast Asia.

Serves 4

PREPARATION TIME
15 minutes

COOKING TIME
5 minutes

1.5kg (3lb 5oz) mussels

1 x 400ml tin of coconut milk

2 tbsp chopped lemongrass

Juice of 2 limes

4 tbsp fish sauce (nam pla)

2 tbsp soft light brown sugar

6 spring onions, trimmed and sliced

4 tbsp chopped coriander

* First prepare the mussels. Rinse the shells in cold running water a couple of times to wash away any sand or grit. Give them a scrub to dislodge any barnacles or bits of weed, then remove the 'beard' with a tug or a sharp knife. Be sure to discard any that are open and won't close when tapped against a hard surface.

* Place all the ingredients except the coriander in a large saucepan on a high heat. Bring to the boil, then reduce the heat, cover with a lid and cook for 3–5 minutes or until all the mussels have opened. (Discard any mussels that remain closed after cooking – do not eat these.) Stir in the coriander and serve immediately.

Scallops mornay

This French classic of scallops, white wine and cream beneath a crispy crumb topping is uncompromisingly rich and perfect with mashed potato (see page 314). It's great for a dinner party or as a substantial starter. It can be prepared in advance and stored for up to 24 hours in the fridge or for a couple of months in the freezer.

Serves 4–6

PREPARATION TIME
10 minutes

COOKING TIME
10–15 minutes

50g (2oz) butter

250g (9oz) button mushrooms, thinly sliced

Salt and freshly ground black pepper

2 tbsp plain flour

250ml (9fl oz) white wine

250ml (9fl oz) single or regular cream

250ml (9fl oz) chicken or fish stock

350g (12oz) shelled scallops (about 8 scallops in total), trimmed and quartered

2 tsp chopped thyme leaves

1 tbsp chopped chives

For the crumb topping

25g (1oz) butter

50g (2oz) fresh white breadcrumbs

50g (2oz) Cheddar cheese, grated

* Melt the butter in a saucepan on a high heat and when the butter starts to foam add the mushrooms and sauté for 2–3 minutes or until tender and lightly golden. Season with salt and pepper.

* Stir in the flour over the heat for 1 minute before gradually pouring in the wine, stirring or gently whisking to remove any lumps in the mixture. Bring to the boil, allowing it to bubble for a couple of minutes, then pour in the cream and stock. Bring back up to the boil, then add the scallops, reduce the heat and simmer for 2–3 minutes or until the scallops are cooked through. Add the herbs and season with salt and pepper to taste. Remove from the heat and set aside.

* Preheat the grill to high.

* To make the crumb topping, melt the butter in a small saucepan, then remove from the heat and stir in the breadcrumbs and grated cheese.

* Pour the scallop mixture into 4–6 gratin dishes or one large ovenproof dish and top with the crumb topping, then place under the hot grill for 3–4 minutes or until bubbling and golden on top.

Variation

Prawns mornay: Make as in the recipe above, simply substituting the scallops with the same quantity of raw langoustines or king prawns, halved.

Thai steamed fish

Steaming is a good way of making sure fish stays perfectly moist. If you don't have a steamer, use a metal sieve instead, covering it with foil or a lid to stop any steam escaping. The Thai flavourings make this dish (and the kitchen!) smell amazing.

Serves 4

PREPARATION TIME
10 minutes

COOKING TIME
10 minutes

4 x 175g (6oz) salmon fillets

2 pak choi, each quartered lengthways

Small handful of coriander leaves

For the sauce

2 tbsp chopped coriander

1 large clove of garlic, peeled and finely grated

2 tbsp fish sauce (nam pla)

2 tsp peeled and finely grated root ginger

2 tbsp lemon juice

* Place all the ingredients for the sauce in a bowl and mix them together.

* Set a vegetable steamer or metal sieve over a saucepan of boiling water. Line the steamer or sieve with a piece of foil or parchment paper (large enough to come just over the edge of the steamer), then place the salmon inside along with the pak choi.

* Drizzle over the sauce, then cover with a piece of foil or a lid and steam for 7–8 minutes or until the fish and pak choi are just tender.

* Transfer the cooked fish and pak choi to warmed plates, saving all the juice, then pour the sauce over the top, followed by a scattering of coriander leaves. Serve on a bed of boiled rice (see page 332).

Chicken stir-fry

It's central to Chinese cuisine that you should never need to use a knife or chop anything up at the table. Hence the cook does all the chopping beforehand, usually before the food is cooked. This does mean that everything cooks extremely quickly in a wok that's good and hot.

Serves 4–6

PREPARATION TIME
10–15 minutes

COOKING TIME
10–15 minutes

4 tbsp unsalted cashew nuts

2 skinless chicken breasts, cut into thin strips

100ml (3½fl oz) Chinese rice wine

2 tsp sesame oil

3 tbsp soy sauce

4 tbsp sunflower oil

6 cloves of garlic, peeled and finely chopped

1 tbsp peeled and finely chopped root ginger

200g (7oz) oyster, shiitake or button mushrooms, quartered

1 red pepper, deseeded and cut into 1cm (½in) dice

½ Savoy cabbage, core removed and leaves shredded crossways (50g/2oz prepared weight)

8 spring onions, trimmed and sliced at an angle

* Place the cashew nuts in a small frying pan on a high heat and cook, tossing frequently, for about 1 minute or until they are browned, then set aside.

* In a bowl, mix together the chicken strips with the rice wine, sesame oil and 2 teaspoons of the soy sauce, then set aside.

* Place a wok or large frying pan on a high heat and allow it to get very hot. Pour in the sunflower oil and, when it is hot, add the garlic and ginger and stir-fry for 30 seconds, then add the mushrooms and red pepper and stir-fry for a further 3–5 minutes.

* Tip in the prepared chicken and cook for 2–3 minutes. Next, add the cabbage and cashew nuts and stir together for another minute, then turn off the heat and stir in the spring onions and the remaining soy sauce. Have a taste, adding more soy sauce if needed, then serve immediately with boiled rice (see page 332) or noodles.

Chicken paillard with creamy cucumber and courgettes

Paillard is a method of preparing a chicken breast that makes cooking it much faster. By cutting the breast almost in half and then opening it out, much more of the meat is exposed to the heat and it will take only a couple of minutes on each side to cook. Here the chicken is served with fresh-tasting cucumber and courgettes in a deliciously creamy sauce.

Serves 4

PREPARATION TIME
10 minutes

COOKING TIME
10 minutes

4 skinless, boneless chicken breasts

Salt and freshly ground black pepper

110g (4oz) butter

400g (14oz) courgette, grated

400g (14oz) cucumber, grated

150ml (5fl oz) single or regular cream

4 tbsp chopped basil or marjoram

* To prepare the chicken, carefully cut each breast almost in half lengthways, then open out the two halves like a book. Season each breast with salt and pepper on both sides.

* Melt half the butter in a frying pan on a high heat and when the butter starts to foam add the chicken breasts. Fry for 2 minutes on each side or until the chicken is opaque all the way through, then allow to rest in a warm place. Transfer to a warmed plate, cover with foil and set aside to rest.

* Add the rest of the butter to the same frying pan on a medium heat and use a wooden spoon to scrape off the bits of browned meat left in the bottom of the pan, stirring them in with the melted butter. Add the courgette and cucumber, season with a little salt and pepper and sauté for about 1 minute, then pour in the cream. Bring to a simmer, cooking for a further 1–2 minutes or until the cream thickens slightly, then stir in the herbs. Pour the sauce over the chicken breasts and serve immediately.

Chicken skewers with carrot and apple salad

This yoghurt and spice mix works as a marinade as well as flavouring the chicken while it cooks. The carrot and apple salad, with its dressing of lemon juice and chopped mint, provides a suitably zingy foil to the tender, spicy meat.

Serves 4

PREPARATION TIME
**10 minutes,
plus marinating**

COOKING TIME
8–10 minutes

4 skinless, boneless chicken breasts, cut into 2cm (¾in) cubes

Salt and freshly ground black pepper

For the marinade

Juice of 2 limes

2 tsp ground cumin

2 tsp ground coriander

4 cloves of garlic, peeled and crushed or finely grated

4 tsp peeled and finely grated root ginger

4 tbsp natural yoghurt

For the carrot and apple salad

2 carrots, peeled and grated

2 eating apples (unpeeled), grated

4 tsp runny honey

Juice of ½ lemon

2 tbsp chopped mint

4–8 wooden or metal skewers

* If using wooden skewers, place the skewers in a bowl, cover with boiling water and leave to soak to prevent them burning during cooking.

* In a bowl, mix together the ingredients for the marinade, then add the chicken pieces and season with salt and pepper. Stir to coat the chicken in the marinade. Cover the bowl with a plate and leave to marinate for 10 minutes.

* As the chicken marinates, mix together the salad ingredients in another bowl, season to taste with salt and pepper and set aside.

* Take the chicken pieces out of the marinade and thread them onto the skewers. Place a frying pan on a medium–low heat, add the chicken skewers and cook for 4–5 minutes on each side or until the meat is opaque all the way through. Place on plates, divide the salad between the dishes and serve.

Pan-fried chicken with mango salsa

Mango is fantastic in a salsa: its sweet juiciness marries so well with the heat of the chilli and the sharpness of the lime juice. I've also added a little crunch with a handful of salted peanuts.

Serves 4

PREPARATION TIME
10 minutes

COOKING TIME
5 minutes

4 skinless, boneless chicken breasts

Salt and freshly ground black pepper

Olive oil, for drizzling

For the Thai mango salsa

1 mango (about 250g/9oz), peeled, stone removed and flesh cut into 1cm (½in) dice

2 spring onions, trimmed and chopped

50g (2oz) salted peanuts, roughly chopped

1 tbsp chopped mint

1 tbsp chopped coriander

¼ red chilli, deseeded and finely chopped

1 tbsp lime juice

1 tbsp fish sauce (nam pla)

1 tbsp caster sugar

* Place all the ingredients for the salsa in a bowl and mix together, then set aside.

* To prepare the chicken, carefully cut each breast almost in half lengthways, then open out the two halves like a book. Season each breast with salt and pepper on both sides and drizzle with just enough olive oil to coat it.

* Place a frying pan or griddle pan on a high heat and allow it to get hot, then add the chicken breasts and cook for about 2 minutes on each side or until the chicken is opaque all the way through. Remove from the pan and serve with the salsa and boiled rice (see page 332) or noodles.

Variation

Pan-fried chicken with watermelon and mint salsa: Prepare and cook the chicken as above but serving it instead with a salsa made from mixing together 200g (7oz) watermelon, peeled and cut into 1cm (½ in) dice, 1 tablespoon of lime juice, 1 tablespoon of chopped mint and 50g (2oz) pine nuts (having toasted these first in a dry frying pan).

Chicken noodle stir-fry

Rice noodles are a really useful 'fast' food as they don't need cooking, just soaking in boiling water. As with any stir-fry, it's important to allow your wok or frying pan to get very hot before you add anything. One way to tell that the wok is hot enough is by listening – as you add more ingredients and keep stir-frying them, they should never stop sizzling.

Serves 2–3

PREPARATION TIME
**10 minutes,
plus soaking**

COOKING TIME
5 minutes

200g (7oz) fine or medium rice noodles

2 tbsp sunflower oil

3 cloves of garlic, peeled and finely chopped

1 tbsp peeled and finely grated root ginger

6 spring onions, trimmed and sliced at an angle

200g (7oz) carrots, peeled and sliced at an angle

2 skinless, boneless chicken breasts (about 300g/11oz in total), cut into 1cm (½in) thick slices

1 x 400ml tin of coconut milk

1 tbsp fish sauce (nam pla)

Small handful of coriander leaves, to serve

* Place the rice noodles in a bowl, cover with boiling water and allow to soak for 4–5 minutes, or according to the instructions on the packet, until softened.

* Place a wok or frying pan on a high heat and allow it to get very hot. Pour in the sunflower oil and when it is hot, add the garlic, ginger and half the spring onions. Stir-fry for 30 seconds, then add the carrots and cook for a further minute. Stir in the chicken and cook for another 2–3 minutes or until the meat is opaque all the way through.

* Stir in the coconut milk and fish sauce, bring to a simmer and allow to bubble for 2 minutes, then drain the noodles and add to the wok or pan. Remove the wok from the heat and stir in the remaining spring onions. Divide between warmed bowls and serve with some coriander leaves.

Pan-fried duck breasts with redcurrant jelly sauce

With a perfectly crispy skin and juicy pink meat, duck breasts are a short-cut to luxury. The sauce is quick to make but richly flavoured. The sweetness of the redcurrant jelly is cut through by the acidity of the vinegar. If you don't have redcurrant jelly, strained blackberry or raspberry jam will do just as well.

Serves 4

PREPARATION TIME
5 minutes

COOKING TIME
20–25 minutes

4 duck breasts (with the skin and fat left on)

Salt and freshly ground black pepper

For the redcurrant jelly sauce

2 shallots or 1 red onion, peeled and finely chopped

6 tbsp redcurrant jelly

2 tbsp red wine vinegar

Juice of 2 oranges

* Using a sharp knife, score the duck breasts with 3 long cuts, diagonally, at 2.5cm (1in) intervals through the skin, but not the meat. Repeat crossways to form a grid pattern. Season on both sides with salt and pepper.

* Place a frying pan on a medium heat, immediately add the duck breasts, skin side down, and after 2 minutes turn the heat down to low. Continue to cook, pouring off the fat every so often into a bowl (see also the tip below), for 10–15 minutes or until the skin is crisp. Increase the heat to medium and turn over the duck breasts. Cook for 4–6 minutes, depending on the thickness of the breasts and how cooked you like the duck, then turn off the heat and allow to rest for a few minutes before serving.

* Meanwhile, make the sauce. Add 2–3 tablespoons of the duck fat to a frying pan and place on a medium heat. Tip in the shallots or onion and cook for 5 minutes or until softened but not browned, then stir in the jelly, vinegar and orange juice. Allow to bubble and reduce for 3–5 minutes or until the mixture is syrupy in consistency. Season with salt and pepper to taste, adding more jelly or vinegar if necessary.

* Serve the duck breasts either whole or cut into slices, and drizzled with the sauce.

Rachel's tip

You can pour any leftover duck fat into a screw-top jar and keep in the fridge for future use. It's perfect for basting roast potatoes!

Lamb chops with parsley and mint sauce

This sauce is such an easy way of adding flavour to lamb chops. The colour is a brilliant green and the sharp, intense flavour works to perfection with the lamb. You can make the sauce the day ahead if needed and store it covered in the fridge.

Serves 4–6

PREPARATION TIME
5 minutes

COOKING TIME
10 minutes

8–12 lamb chops

4 tbsp olive oil

Salt and freshly ground black pepper

For the parsley and mint sauce

Handful of mint leaves

2 handfuls of parsley leaves

2 tbsp capers, drained and rinsed

8 tinned anchovies

6 tbsp olive oil

2–4 tbsp lemon juice

* First make the sauce. Place the herbs, capers, anchovies, olive oil and 2 tablespoons of the lemon juice in a food processor. Whiz for a minute, then add salt and pepper or more lemon juice to taste. If you don't have a food processor you can chop everything finely by hand and mix together.

* Place a frying pan or griddle pan on a high heat. While it is heating, drizzle the lamb chops with the olive oil and season with salt and pepper, then place in the hot pan and cook for 2–4 minutes on each side until just pink in the centre. Serve immediately with a drizzling of the sauce and a salad or mash. For a great spring meal, you can serve with the Roasted New Potatoes (see page 313) and the Sticky Roast Carrots in Maple Syrup (see page 329).

Pork stir-fry

Pork tenderloin is a fantastic cut of meat – lean, beautifully tender and takes only minutes to cook. Here it is served in a piquant sauce that offers my take on the classic Chinese combination of sweet and sour.

Serves 4

PREPARATION TIME
10 minutes

COOKING TIME
10 minutes

600g (1lb 5oz) pork tenderloin, cut into 1cm (½in) thick slices

Salt and freshly ground black pepper

2 tbsp sunflower oil

2 cloves of garlic, peeled and crushed or finely grated

1 tsp peeled and finely grated root ginger

3 spring onions, trimmed and sliced at an angle

½ red pepper, deseeded and cut into 5mm (¼in) dice

For the sauce

1 tbsp cider vinegar

3 tbsp soy sauce

1 tbsp tomato purée

2 tbsp Chinese rice wine

2 tsp caster sugar

300ml (½ pint) chicken stock

1 tbsp cornflour

1 tbsp sesame oil

* Place a wok or large frying pan on a high heat and allow to get very hot. While the wok is heating, mix all the sauce ingredients together in a bowl.

* Season the pork with salt and pepper, then add the sunflower oil to the wok or pan. When the oil is hot, tip in the garlic, ginger and spring onions and stir-fry for 30 seconds.

* Add the pork and stir-fry for 2–3 minutes or until it is cooked through, then pour in the sauce along with the red pepper. Bring to the boil and cook for about 3 minutes or until the sauce has thickened slightly. Serve immediately with boiled rice (see page 332).

Pork chops with sage and apple

There are some foods that seem destined to be together. Pork and apples is one such partnership – so happily married, in fact, that they need little encouragement to create something sublime.

Serves 4

PREPARATION TIME
5 minutes

COOKING TIME
15 minutes

30g (1¼oz) butter

2 tbsp olive oil

4 pork loin chops (each about 1.5cm/⅝in thick)

Salt and freshly ground black pepper

2 eating apples, peeled and cut into 5mm (¼in) thick slices

200ml (7fl oz) cider

4 tbsp crème fraîche

4 tsp chopped sage

* Place the butter and olive oil in a large frying pan on a high heat and when the butter has melted and starts to foam, place the chops in the pan and season with salt and pepper. Cook on one side for 2–3 minutes until golden underneath, then turn over and season again.

* Turn over the chops and place the apple slices in the pan, nestling them in among the pork, then cook for about 5 minutes, tossing the slices regularly, until the apples are golden and softened and the chops are cooked through.

* Pour in the cider and stir in the crème fraîche and sage, then bring to a simmer and allow to bubble for a couple of minutes or until slightly thickened. Season with salt and pepper to taste and serve.

Garam masala pork with yoghurt

Garam masala is a spice blend used to add flavour to a whole range of Indian dishes. There is no set recipe, but you can easily make your own with the spices in your cupboard (see below).

Serves 4–6

PREPARATION TIME
10 minutes

COOKING TIME
15 minutes

400g (14oz) pork fillet, trimmed and cut into 1cm (½in) thick slices

1½ tbsp garam masala (bought or homemade, see below)

2 tbsp sunflower oil

2 onions, peeled and finely chopped

4 cloves of garlic, peeled and crushed

½–1 red chilli, deseeded and chopped

Salt and freshly ground black pepper

2 tbsp natural yoghurt

* Place the pork in a bowl with the garam masala and half the oil. Mix together well, then cover the bowl with a plate and set aside.

* Pour the remaining oil into a frying pan on a medium heat and, when hot, add the onions, garlic and chilli, season with salt and pepper and cook for 8–10 minutes or until the onions are soft and lightly browned.

* Season the pork and add to the pan, cooking for 2–3 minutes on each side. Stir in the yoghurt, 1 tablespoon at a time, mixing it in thoroughly, then cook for a further minute. Serve with boiled rice (see page 332).

Homemade garam masala (optional)

20–25 cardamom pods

1 tsp cumin seeds

1 tsp black peppercorns

1 tsp cloves

½ tbsp ground cinnamon

½ tsp freshly grated nutmeg

* Lay the flat side of a large knife over the the cardamom pods on a chopping board and press down to lightly crush. Remove the seeds, discard the pods and grind the seeds, peppercorns and cloves to a powder with a pestle and mortar. Mix with the cinnamon and nutmeg.

Maple black pepper pork chops

With its sweet, highly distinctive flavour, maple syrup is perfect with pork. This recipe is a celebration of that combination – the cider vinegar counterbalances the sweetness of the syrup.

Serves 4

PREPARATION TIME
5 minutes

COOKING TIME
20–25 minutes

4–6 tbsp olive oil

4 pork chops, each about 1.5cm (⅝in) thick

Salt and freshly ground black pepper

2 red onions, peeled and finely chopped

2 tbsp chopped thyme leaves

100ml (3½fl oz) cider vinegar

150ml (5fl oz) maple syrup

* Pour 4 tablespoons of olive oil into a large frying pan (preferably not a non-stick pan as a non-stick pan won't catch the browned pieces of pork, which are essential for this sauce) over a medium heat. Season the pork chops all over with 2 teaspoons of salt and, when the oil is hot, add these to the pan.

* Cook for 3–5 minutes on each side, depending on how thick the chops are; they should be nicely browned on each side and cooked all the way through. Transfer from the pan onto a warmed plate, then cover with foil and place somewhere warm.

* If there isn't much oil left in the pan, add the extra tablespoon, then tip in the onions and thyme leaves. Season with more salt, then stir-fry for about 3 minutes or until the onions have softened but not browned.

* Pour in the vinegar, using a wooden spoon to scrape off and stir in the browned bits from the bottom of the pan. Bring to a simmer and cook for a further 2 minutes, then stir in the maple syrup and 1 teaspoon of pepper.

* Bring to a simmer once again and cook for 7–10 minutes or until the sauce has reduced to a sticky glaze. Taste for seasoning, then pour the sauce over the pork chops and serve with mashed potatoes (see page 314) and some blanched kale.

Seared beef salad

Thinly sliced fillet steak makes a tender and juicy basis for a salad. The sweet roasted onions and salty blue cheese turn this into something seriously impressive.

Serves 4

PREPARATION TIME
10 minutes

COOKING TIME
15–20 minutes

2 red onions, peeled and cut through the root into 6 wedges

2 tbsp olive oil, plus extra for drizzling

1 tsp thyme leaves

Salt and freshly ground black pepper

2 tsp balsamic vinegar

4 handfuls of mixed salad leaves

300g (11oz) beef fillet, cut into 12 thin slices

50g (2oz) blue cheese, roughly crumbled

For the dressing

3 tbsp olive oil

2 tsp balsamic vinegar

2 tsp Dijon mustard

* Preheat the oven to 220°C (425°F), Gas mark 7.

* Place the onion wedges in a roasting tin, then drizzle with the 2 tablespoons of olive oil and sprinkle over the thyme. Season with salt and pepper and roast in the oven for 15–20 minutes or until tender and caramelised at the edges. Remove from the oven and sprinkle over the balsamic vinegar.

* While the onions are cooking, make the dressing by mixing all the ingredients together and seasoning with salt and pepper.

* Just before the onions have finished cooking, place a griddle pan or frying pan on a high heat and while the pan heats up, toss the salad leaves in the dressing and divide between plates.

* Drizzle the beef with a little olive oil and season with salt and pepper, then when the pan is very hot, add the meat and cook for about 30 seconds on each side (or longer if you prefer).

* Once the beef is cooked to your liking, place 3 slices on each plate next to the salad, along with 3 wedges of roasted red onion. Finally, scatter over the blue cheese and serve.

Stir-fried steak with kale

A staple of Chinese cooking, oyster sauce is made by reducing oyster cooking water until it has thickened and caramelised to a deep brown colour. The result is an intense savoury sauce that goes especially well with beef. It is available from Asian food shops and most big supermarkets.

Serves 2–3

PREPARATION TIME
10 minutes

COOKING TIME
10 minutes

1 tbsp cornflour

3 tbsp oyster sauce

3 tbsp soy sauce

500g (1lb 2oz) trimmed rump steak, cut into thin strips

2 tbsp groundnut oil

150ml (5fl oz) chicken or vegetable stock

100g (3½oz) (prepared weight) kale leaves, stalks and centre ribs removed and leaves shredded

6 spring onions, trimmed and sliced at an angle

25g (1oz) salted peanuts, roughly chopped, to serve

* In a bowl, mix together the cornflour with 2 tablespoons each of the oyster and soy sauces, then stir in the steak.

* Pour the groundnut oil into a wok or frying pan on a high heat and allow it to get very hot. Tip in the beef slices and stir-fry for 2–3 minutes or until the meat is cooked through. Remove from the pan and set aside.

* Pour in the stock, then bring to the boil and stir in the kale. Cook for 2–3 minutes or until the kale is tender, then stir in the cooked beef and the spring onions. Season with the remaining oyster and soy sauces to taste, then serve with boiled rice (see page 332) and a scattering of the peanuts.

Spiced apples and pears

Lightly pan-fried apples and pears, spiced with cinnamon, make a simple but effective accompaniment for ice cream or yoghurt.

Serves 4 (v)

PREPARATION TIME
5 minutes

COOKING TIME
10–15 minutes

25g (1oz) butter

1 eating apple, peeled, cored and cut into 5mm (¼in) thick slices

1 pear, peeled, cored and cut into 5mm (¼in) thick slices

1 tbsp soft light brown sugar

1 tsp ground cinnamon

Pinch of salt

75ml (3fl oz) single or regular cream

* Melt the butter in a frying pan on a medium–high heat and, when foaming, add the apple and pear. Sauté, tossing frequently, for 5 minutes, then stir in the sugar, cinnamon and a pinch of salt and cook for a further 5–7 minutes or until soft and lightly browned.

* Stir in the cream and 1 tablespoon of water, allow the mixture to bubble for just 30 seconds, then serve over ice cream or with natural yoghurt.

Baked peaches with honey and pecans

Peaches or nectarines work equally well in this recipe.

Serves 4 (v)

PREPARATION TIME
2 minutes

COOKING TIME
12–14 minutes

4 peaches (unpeeled) or nectarines, halved and stones removed

50g (2oz) butter, softened

4 tbsp runny honey

50g (2oz) shelled pecan nuts, roughly chopped

* Preheat the oven to 180°C (350°F), Gas mark 4.
* Place the peaches or nectarines, skin side down on, on a baking tray. Spread with the butter, then drizzle over the honey and scatter with the pecans.
* Place in the oven and bake for 12–14 minutes or until the peaches or nectarines are soft and lightly browned. Serve immediately with vanilla ice cream or some whipped cream or crème fraîche.

Coconut macaroon meringue

Both crisp and chewy, this meringue is incredibly easy to make and yet absolutely delicious. Sticking to the tropical theme, I've topped it with cubes of soft sweet mango tossed in fresh lime juice and resting on a layer of whipped cream. Irresistible!

Serves 6–8 (v)

PREPARATION TIME
10 minutes

COOKING TIME
20 minutes, plus cooling

1 ripe mango

Juice of 1 lime

150ml (5fl oz) double or regular cream

A few mint leaves, to decorate (optional)

For the coconut macaroon meringue

3 egg whites

175g (6oz) desiccated coconut

125g (4½oz) caster sugar

* Preheat the oven to 180°C (350°F), Gas mark 4. Line a baking sheet with baking parchment.

* To make the meringue, place the egg whites in a spotlessly clean bowl and lightly whisk until frothy but not yet forming soft peaks. Then mix in the desiccated coconut and sugar with a metal spoon.

* Tip the mixture out onto the prepared baking sheet and shape into a round about 22cm (8½ in) in diameter, making sure the centre is slightly hollowed out (to hold the mango and whipped cream).

* Bake for about 18 minutes or until the meringue is a rich golden brown (but not burnt!). Remove from the oven and leave to stand for a few minutes on the baking sheet, then place a wire rack on top of the meringue and flip over so that it is upside down. Peel off the baking parchment and allow to cool. Once cool, flip the meringue over onto a serving plate so that it is the right way up again.

* While the meringue is cooling, peel the mango, remove the stone and cut the flesh into 1–2cm (½–¾ in) cubes. Place in a bowl, add the lime juice and toss together.

* Pour the cream into another bowl and whisk until it forms soft peaks, then spread over the cooled meringue. Arrange the pieces of mango on the top of the whipped cream and decorate with a few mint leaves (if using) to serve.

Banoffee pancakes

Light and fluffy pancakes obviously make a great breakfast. But served here with sliced bananas, toffee sauce and cream or ice cream, they make a gorgeous and quite substantial dessert.

**Makes about
10 pancakes (v)**

PREPARATION TIME
10 minutes

COOKING TIME
15 minutes

150g (5oz) self-raising flour

1–2 tbsp caster sugar

1 egg, lightly beaten

150ml (5fl oz) milk

15g (½oz) butter (optional)

To serve

3 bananas, peeled and sliced

Ice cream or whipped cream

200ml (7fl oz) toffee sauce (see page 58) or dulce de leche (or boiled condensed milk, see recipe introduction, page 46)

* Sift the flour into a bowl, add the sugar and mix together. In a separate bowl, whisk together the egg and milk, then make a well in the centre of the dry ingredients, pour in the liquid and mix until just combined. (Be careful not to over-stir or the finished pancakes will taste tough.)

* Melt about a third of the butter (if using) in a small frying pan on a medium–low heat and when the butter starts to foam add generous tablespoons of the batter to the pan to form 3–4 pancakes. (If you're using a non-stick pan, then it isn't necessary to include butter.) Cook for about 2 minutes or until bubbles appear on the surface of the pancakes, by which time they should be golden brown underneath.

* Turn the pancakes over and cook until they feel set in the centre and both sides are golden brown. Repeat with the rest of the mixture, adding more butter as necessary. Transfer the finished pancakes to a warmed plate, cover with an upturned bowl or some foil and keep warm in a low oven.

* Serve the pancakes scattered with slices of banana, a few blobs of ice cream or whipped cream and a drizzling of warm toffee sauce or dulce de leche.

Quick blueberry trifles

These super-speedy desserts are light and summery without any of the heaviness of a traditional boozy trifle.

Serves 4 (v)

PREPARATION TIME
10 minutes

COOKING TIME
5 minutes

150g (5oz) fresh or frozen blueberries

100g (3½oz) caster sugar

Juice of ½ lemon

1 egg, separated

125g (4½oz) mascarpone

8 Rich Tea biscuits, broken into bite-sized pieces

Four glasses

* Place the blueberries in a saucepan, along with half the sugar, the lemon juice and 50ml (2fl oz) water. Bring to the boil, then reduce the heat and simmer, stirring occasionally, for 3–4 minutes or until soft. Remove from the heat and allow to cool in the pan.

* In a spotlessly clean bowl, whisk the egg white until it forms stiff peaks. Place the egg yolk in another bowl, add the remaining caster sugar and the mascarpone and whisk together for 1 minute or until combined, then fold in the whisked egg white.

* Pour the cooled blueberries into a sieve set over a bowl for the juices to drain into, then tip the berries from the sieve into another bowl.

* Place the biscuit pieces into the blueberry liquid to soak for a few seconds. Spoon these into the glasses, then add half the berries, followed by half the mascarpone mixture, dividing them between the glasses.

* Soak the remaining biscuits in the blueberry liquid and divide between the glasses, along with the remaining berries and the last of the mascarpone mixture. If there's any liquid left, this can be drizzled over the top of the trifles. Serve immediately or keep covered in the fridge (for several hours or overnight) until you are ready to serve.

Chocolate mascarpone mousse

I adore this seriously rich and divinely velvety dessert. It is perfect if you want something special to round off a meal but need to knock it up at the last minute. If you have more time, or prefer the mousse to be chilled and more set, it can be kept in the fridge for a few hours or overnight.

Serves 4–6 (v)

PREPARATION TIME
10 minutes

COOKING TIME
5 minutes

100g (3½oz) dark chocolate, broken into pieces, or dark chocolate drops

75g (3oz) caster sugar

2–3 tbsp brandy

2 eggs

250g (9oz) mascarpone

4–6 glasses, cups or bowls

* Place the chocolate in a heatproof bowl set over a saucepan of simmering water and allow to melt, then remove from the heat.

* Add the sugar, brandy and eggs and, using a hand-held electric beater, whisk for 5 minutes or until the outside of the bowl has cooled down to tepid.

* Whisk in the mascarpone for a few seconds, just until combined. (The mousse will thicken once the mascarpone has been mixed in.) Divide between the glasses, cups or bowls and serve straightaway or chill to use later.

Baked white chocolate vanilla custards

White chocolate is made without cocoa solids and I love the sweet chocolatey-vanilla taste it brings to desserts. These baked custards are quick to make and delicious on their own, though in the summer I like to serve them with fresh raspberries or strawberries.

Serves 6 (v)

PREPARATION TIME
5 minutes

COOKING TIME
25–30 minutes

150ml (5fl oz) milk

250ml (9fl oz) double or regular cream

150g (5oz) white chocolate, broken into pieces, or white chocolate drops

4 eggs

1 tsp vanilla extract

Icing sugar, for dusting (optional)

Six 100ml (3½fl oz) ramekins

* Preheat the oven to 160°C (325°F), Gas mark 3.

* Pour the milk and cream into a saucepan and bring to the boil. Remove from the heat, tip in the chocolate and stir to melt completely.

* Crack the eggs into a bowl, add the vanilla extract and whisk together, then pour the chocolate cream onto the beaten eggs, whisking thoroughly to mix.

* Pour the mixture into the ramekins, place in a bain-marie (a roasting tin filled to a depth of about 2cm/¾in with boiling water) and bake in the oven for 20–25 minutes until the custards are just set in the middle. (They are ready when a skewer inserted into the centre of each dish comes out clean.)

* Serve hot or at room temperature. These are lovely served with a dusting of icing sugar, if you like, and some fresh strawberries.

Quick fruit brûlée

I use a mixture of peaches or nectarines, bananas and strawberries for my fruit brulée, but what I love about this completely fuss free-dessert is that it can be made with whatever fruit you have.

Serves 4 (v)

PREPARATION TIME
**10 minutes,
plus chilling**

COOKING TIME
12 minutes

100g (3½oz) caster sugar, plus 1 tbsp for sweetening

2 bananas, peeled and cut at an angle into 5mm (¼in) thick slices

4 nectarines, stones removed and flesh cut into wedges 5mm (¼in) thick

16 strawberries, hulled and quartered

1 tbsp caster sugar

1 tbsp lemon juice

4 tbsp mascarpone or whipped cream

* In a large bowl, toss the fruit with the 1 tablespoon caster sugar and lemon juice. Divide between individual bowls, adding a few blobs of the mascarpone or whipped cream to each one.

* Next, make the caramel to go on top. Place the 100g (3½ oz) caster sugar in a small–medium saucepan on a medium heat and stir. It will begin to look lumpy and sandy, but don't worry – just keep stirring. Eventually it will become viscous, turning from a golden to a rich caramel colour. Altogether this can take up to about 12 minutes.

* Using a spoon, carefully drizzle all the caramel over the mascarpone or whipped cream and the fruit. Let the caramel cool and set for about 5 minutes, then serve.

Five Ingredients or Less

We can all feel daunted sometimes by a recipe with two pages worth of ingredients. It isn't necessary to always use many different elements to make great food. These are recipes that need minimal preparation from the shopping to the chopping. They aren't complicated, but by using the right five ingredients you don't have to compromise on flavour.

Do note that because oil, lemon, salt and pepper are staples in so many recipes, and because you're more than likely to have them on hand at all times, I haven't included them in the counting...

Sweet potato and Gruyère tortilla

A take on a classic Spanish tortilla, this baked omelette looks wonderfully dramatic straight from the oven when it's all puffed up and golden. It's great eaten hot, but you can enjoy it at room temperature too which makes it perfect for picnics.

Serves 4–6 (v)

PREPARATION TIME
10 minutes

COOKING TIME
1 hour

2 tbsp olive oil

2 onions, peeled and sliced

Salt and freshly ground black pepper

1–2 sweet potatoes (about 250g/9oz in total), peeled and cut into wedges 1cm (½in) thick

8 eggs

125g (4½oz) Gruyère cheese, grated

25cm (10in) diameter ovenproof frying pan

* Preheat the oven to 200°C (400°F), Gas mark 6.

* Pour the olive oil into the frying pan on a medium–high heat and, when hot, add the onions and season with salt and pepper. Cook for about 10 minutes or until the onions are soft and lightly browned.

* Throw the sweet potatoes into the pan with the onions and roast in the oven for 25–30 minutes, turning occasionally, until tender and golden.

* Crack the eggs into a large bowl, then beat them together thoroughly and season with salt and pepper. Pour the eggs over the cooked sweet potatoes and onions and top with the cheese. Place back in the oven and cook for a further 20 minutes or until the eggs are slightly puffed up and the top is golden and slightly springy to the touch.

* Put the pan on a board and serve the tortilla straight from the pan or carefully slide it onto a serving plate. Cut into wedges and serve with a green salad.

Penne with smoked trout

Trout has a subtle earthy flavour that is enhanced by smoking. Smoked trout is available from fishmongers and some supermarkets, but if you can't find it, smoked mackerel will do just as well in this recipe.

Serves 4

PREPARATION TIME
5 minutes

COOKING TIME
10–12 minutes

Salt and freshly ground black pepper

350g (12oz) dried penne or other pasta, such as fusilli or farfalle

300ml (½ pint) crème fraîche

Juice of 1 lemon

3 tbsp olive oil

225g (8oz) smoked trout or smoked mackerel, skin removed and flesh broken into chunks

1 large avocado (about 200g/7oz), peeled, stone removed and flesh cut into 1cm (½in) dice

* Fill a large saucepan with water, add 1 teaspoon of salt and bring to the boil. Add the pasta and cook for 10–12 minutes, or according to the instructions on the packet, until al dente. Drain the pasta, reserving about 50ml (2fl oz) of the cooking liquid.

* In a bowl, mix together the crème fraîche with the lemon juice and olive oil, then add to the cooked pasta with the reserved cooking liquid and toss together. Carefully fold in the smoked trout or smoked mackerel and the pieces of avocado. Season with salt and pepper to taste and serve.

Conchiglie with spinach, blue cheese and pine nuts

If you can, it's worth using baby spinach for this recipe as the young tender leaves take only a minute or two to wilt in the pan. Any blue cheese works well here, but I particularly like creamy blues such as Gorgonzola or Cashel Blue.

Serves 4–6 (v)

PREPARATION TIME
2 minutes

COOKING TIME
12–15 minutes

Salt and freshly ground black pepper

350g (12oz) dried conchiglie or other pasta, such as fusilli or penne

100g (3½oz) pine nuts

400g (14oz) baby spinach

100g (3½oz) blue cheese, crumbled

* Fill a large saucepan with water, add 1 teaspoon of salt and bring to the boil. Add the pasta and cook for 10–12 minutes, or according to the instructions on the packet, until al dente.

* Meanwhile, toast the pine nuts. Place in a small frying pan on a high heat and cook, tossing frequently, for about 1 minute or until browned (taking care not to let them burn), then set aside.

* Drain the pasta, reserving about 50ml (2fl oz) of the cooking liquid in the pan. Return the cooked pasta to the pan and place on a medium heat. Stir in the spinach, and cook for 1–2 minutes or until the leaves have wilted.

* Tip into a bowl and toss with the blue cheese and toasted pine nuts. Divide between serving bowls, add a grinding of black pepper and serve.

Penne with broad beans and asparagus

I love that time of year when we can get both fresh asparagus and fresh broad beans. When ingredients are this good, it takes very little effort to knock up a memorable meal.

Serves 4–6

PREPARATION TIME
10 minutes

COOKING TIME
10–12 minutes

Salt and freshly ground black pepper

350g (12oz) dried penne or other pasta, such as fusilli or farfalle

250g (9oz) shelled broad beans

250g (9oz) asparagus spears, woody ends snapped off and discarded, cut at an angle into 2cm (¾in) thick slices

75g (3oz) Parmesan cheese, finely grated

Finely grated zest of 1 lemon

4 tbsp olive oil

* Fill a large saucepan with water, add 1 teaspoon of salt and bring to the boil. Add the pasta and cook for 10–12 minutes, or according to the instructions on the packet, until al dente.

* While the pasta is cooking, bring another large saucepan of salted water to the boil. Tip in the broad beans and cook for 2 minutes, then remove from the water with a slotted spoon.

* Add the asparagus to the bean cooking water with a little more salt, bring back up to the boil, then reduce the heat and simmer for about 4–6 minutes depending on size, until just tender.

* While the pasta and asparagus are cooking, press on each of the broad beans with your forefinger to pop them out of their skins. Discard the skins and add the beans to a large bowl. When the asparagus is cooked, drain and add to the same bowl.

* Drain the pasta and add to the beans and asparagus, along with the Parmesan cheese, lemon zest and olive oil. Season with salt and/or pepper to taste, toss everything together and serve.

Fusilli with fried onions and olives

Onions, olives and anchovies are the stars of many Provençal recipes. Here they work their sweet and salty magic on a simple pasta sauce.

Serves 4

PREPARATION TIME
10 minutes

COOKING TIME
20 minutes

4 tbsp olive oil

4 onions, peeled and thinly sliced

Salt and freshly ground black pepper

50g (2oz) pitted and chopped black olives

8 tinned anchovies, chopped

2 tsp finely chopped rosemary leaves

350g (12oz) dried fusilli or other pasta, such as farfalle or conchiglie

* Pour the olive oil into a large frying pan on a medium heat. (The pan should be large enough to hold all the pasta once it is cooked.) When the oil is hot, add the onions and stir together, then season with a little salt and pepper (bearing in mind that the olives and anchovies will be salty). Continue to cook, stirring occasionally, for 15–20 minutes or until the onions are completely soft and golden brown. Then stir in the olives, anchovies and rosemary.

* After the onions have been cooking for 10 minutes, fill a large saucepan with water, add 1 teaspoon of salt and bring to the boil. Add the fusilli and cook for 10–12 minutes, or according to the instructions on the packet, until al dente.

* When the pasta has finished cooking, drain, then stir into the onion mixture. Add a grinding of black pepper and serve.

Fish baked with potatoes

With the potatoes and fish roasted simply in olive oil, and the onions deliciously caramelised, this can be described as a healthy take on deep-fried fish and chips.

Serves 4

PREPARATION TIME
10 minutes

COOKING TIME
35–45 minutes

4 floury potatoes (about 600g/1lb 5oz in total), peeled and cut into 2cm (¾in) dice

2 red onions, peeled and cut through the root into 8 wedges

100ml (3½fl oz) olive oil, plus extra for drizzling

Salt and freshly ground black pepper

4 white fish fillets (about 150g/5oz each), such as pollock, haddock or cod

4 lemon wedges, to serve

* Preheat the oven to 220°C (425°F), Gas mark 7.

* In a large bowl, toss together the potatoes and onions with the olive oil and season with salt and pepper. Place in a roasting tin and roast in the oven for 20–25 minutes, tossing a couple of times, until the potatoes are a light golden colour and beginning to get crispy.

* Season the fish on both sides with salt and pepper, then drizzle a little olive oil over each fillet. Place on top of the potatoes and onions, then return to the oven and cook for a further 12–18 minutes or until the fish is opaque all the way through. Serve immediately with wedges of lemon.

Fish *en papillote*, three ways

Papillote means 'parchment' in French. By cooking fish in a parcel of baking parchment all the flavours and moisture are sealed in. I have given you three variations here, each of which can be served straight from the oven in their parcels on warmed plates. As you open each parcel, their gorgeous aromas are released.

Each recipe below and on page 164 serves 1

PREPARATION TIME
10 minutes, plus marinating for the Thai-flavoured Fish (next page)

COOKING TIME
12–14 minutes

Making a *papillote*

* For each serving cut out a piece of baking parchment or foil measuring about 30cm (12in) square.

* Add your fish and other ingredients to the parchment square, placing them to one side of the centre of the piece of paper.

* Fold the square in half to enclose the filling and then fold in the edges to seal and form a parcel. The finished parcel should be semi-circular in shape, looking rather like a Cornish pasty.

Salmon and mascarpone and peas

2 tsp mascarpone

1 tbsp single or regular cream

35g (1¼oz) frozen peas

Squeeze of lemon juice

Salt and freshly ground black pepper

125g (4½oz) salmon fillet, skin removed

* Preheat the oven to 220°C (425°F), Gas mark 7.

* In a bowl, mix together the mascarpone and cream, then stir in the peas and season with lemon juice, salt and pepper. Place this mixture on the square of baking parchment, put the fish on top and fold up to form a parcel (see above).

* Place the parcels on a baking sheet and cook in the oven for 12–14 minutes or until the salmon is just opaque all the way through.

En papillote recipes continued on the next page...

Fish *en papillote* (cont.)

Salmon with tomato and basil

4–6 thin slices of tomato

Salt and freshly ground black pepper

2 pinches of granulated or caster sugar

3–4 basil leaves

6 thin slices of cucumber

125g (4½oz) salmon fillet, skin removed

10g (⅓oz) butter

* Preheat the oven to 220°C (425°F), Gas mark 7.

* Place the tomatoes on the square of baking parchment (see page 162), season with salt, pepper and a pinch of sugar, then add the basil leaves followed by the cucumber. Next, place the salmon fillet on top, followed by the butter.

* Season again with salt and pepper and sugar and fold the baking parchment to form a parcel as on page 162. Place on a baking sheet and cook in the oven for 12–14 minutes or until the salmon is just opaque all the way through.

Thai-flavoured fish

¼ tsp peeled and grated root ginger

1 tsp soy sauce

Juice of ½ lemon

2 spring onions, trimmed and sliced

1 tsp soft light brown sugar

125g (4½oz) white fish fillet, such as pollock, haddock or cod

Salt and freshly ground black pepper

* Preheat the oven to 220°C (425°F), Gas mark 7.

* In a bowl, mix together the ginger, soy sauce, lemon juice, spring onions and sugar. Add the fish and allow to marinate for 15 minutes, during which time the fish will darken.

* Place the marinated fish onto the parchment square (see page 162) and pour over the remaining liquid with the spring onions. Season, if you like, with a tiny amount of salt and pepper (bearing in mind that the soy sauce is salty), then fold up to form a parcel, as on page 162.

* Place on a baking sheet and cook in the oven for 10–12 minutes or until the fish is just opaque all the way through.

Mackerel with chorizo

Mackerel has a distinctive taste that stands up well to foods with an equally strong flavour, such as the chorizo used here. Fish is always better the fresher it is, and this is especially true with mackerel. Select fish that are firm, shiny and bright-eyed.

Serves 4

PREPARATION TIME
10 minutes

COOKING TIME
10 minutes

4 whole mackerel (with the skin left on), heads removed

4 tbsp olive oil

12 cloves of garlic, peeled and left whole

150g (5oz) chorizo, cut into 1cm (½in) pieces

Salt and freshly ground black pepper

Juice of 1 lemon

100ml (3½fl oz) water or white wine

4 tbsp chopped parsley

Lemon wedges, to serve

* Using a sharp knife, slash the skin of the mackerel at an angle on each side 3 times, each slash evenly spaced and just a few millimetres deep.

* Pour the olive oil into a large frying pan on a medium heat and, when hot, add the garlic and chorizo. Fry, stirring occasionally, for 2–3 minutes or until the garlic has turned a pale golden colour (but making sure it doesn't burn) and the chorizo has released its deep amber oils. Remove from the pan (leaving any oil behind) and set aside.

* Add the mackerel to the pan and season with salt and pepper. Fry the fish for about 2 minutes on each side or until the skin has browned, then add the cooked chorizo and garlic with the lemon juice and water or wine, cover with a lid and reduce the heat to low.

* Cook for a further 4–5 minutes or until the fish is just opaque all the way through and the meat lifts easily from the bone. Transfer to warmed plates, divide the chorizo and garlic between the fish and drizzle over the sauce, then sprinkle with the chopped parsley and serve with a lemon wedge on the side.

Fennel baked fish

The aniseed notes of fennel work particularly well with white fish, while the addition of a little cream combines the cooked juices from both into a quick but delicious sauce.

Serves 4

PREPARATION TIME
5 minutes

COOKING TIME
30 minutes

1 large fennel bulb, trimmed, reserving the fronds

4 sprigs of fennel, dill, tarragon or chervil

4 x 150g (5oz) skinless white fish fillets, such as pollock, haddock, cod or hake

75ml (3fl oz) white wine

Salt and freshly ground black pepper

50ml (2fl oz) double or regular cream

* Preheat the oven to 180°C (350°F), Gas mark 4.

* Cut the fennel bulb lengthways into thin slices, each about 3mm (⅛in) thick. Spread these out in a gratin or ovenproof dish, lay the herbs on top, spacing them evenly, and cover each sprig with a portion of fish.

* Pour the wine over the fish, then season with salt and pepper, cover with foil and bake in the oven for about 20 minutes or until the fish is opaque all the way through.

* When the fish is cooked, take the dish out of the oven and carefully pour the juices into a small saucepan, then place the foil back over the fish and return the dish to the oven (with the heat turned off) to keep warm.

* Place the saucepan on a high heat, stir in the cream and bring to the boil, allowing it to bubble away for 4–5 minutes or until the sauce is slightly thickened. To serve, divide the fennel between plates and add a piece of fish to each plate, then pour over the sauce and decorate with the reserved fennel fronds.

Spicy squid salad

The texture of squid cooked for just a few minutes is soft and yielding with a unique flavour; never cook for longer than that or it becomes rubbery. I like to cook it in a hot griddle pan or on a barbecue, where the fiery heat crisps and slightly chars the squid, intensifying the flavour. Smoked paprika is a perfect sweet spice to serve with fish and goes especially well with the tomatoes in this salad.

Serves 2–4

PREPARATION TIME
10 minutes

COOKING TIME
4–8 minutes

2 squid (about 350g/12oz total prepared weight – see method)

4 tbsp olive oil

2 tsp smoked paprika

Salt and freshly ground black pepper

2 tbsp capers, rinsed

4 handfuls of rocket leaves

2 tomatoes, cut into 1cm (½in) dice, or 12 cherry tomatoes, quartered

Squeeze of lemon juice, plus lemon wedges to serve

* If your fishmonger hasn't already cleaned the squid, rinse each one in water and, holding the body in one hand and the tentacles in the other, carefully pull the tentacles and gut away from the body in one piece. Remove the wings, retaining these, then feel inside the body for the hard quill and pull this out and discard.

* Using a sharp knife, make a cut down one side of the body and open out flat. Scrape away any traces of gut with your knife, then lightly score the flesh in a criss-cross pattern. Do the same to the wings, then cut both these and the body into pieces roughly 3cm (1¼ in) square. Cut the tentacles away from the gut, discarding this, and slice these in half.

* In a bowl, mix together half the olive oil with the paprika and season with salt and pepper. Add the prepared squid pieces and mix well.

* Place a griddle or large frying pan on a high heat and allow to get hot. Transfer the squid from the bowl to the hot pan and cook for 2–4 minutes on each side or until slightly browned (and lightly charred if using a griddle pan). Add the capers to the pan for the last 30 seconds of cooking.

* As the squid cooks, place the rocket leaves in another bowl with the tomatoes, lemon juice and remaining olive oil, and toss together, seasoning with salt and pepper. Divide the salad between plates, place the cooked squid on top, along with the capers, add the lemon wedges and serve immediately.

Salmon with capers and dill

The distinctive flavour of dill has a real affinity with fish, particularly salmon. In Scandinavia dill is added to all sorts of dishes, from pickles to gravlax, and is as commonly used as a garnish as parsley is in the rest of Europe.

Serves 4

PREPARATION TIME
5 minutes

COOKING TIME
10 minutes

50g (2oz) butter, diced

4 x 125g (4½oz) salmon fillets (with the skin left on if you wish)

Salt and freshly ground black pepper

4 tbsp capers, drained and rinsed

2 tbsp lemon juice mixed with 6–8 tbsp water

4 tsp chopped dill

* Place a frying pan on a medium–high heat. When it is just hot, add a couple of knobs of butter, very quickly followed by the salmon – with the presentation side down. Fry for 3–4 minutes or until golden brown underneath, then turn over, season with salt and pepper and fry for another couple of minutes or until the fish is just cooked through. (The timing will depend on the thickness of the salmon fillets and heat of the pan.)

* Add the capers, along with the remaining butter and mixed lemon juice and water, and boil for 1 minute. Season to taste, adding more lemon juice or water if necessary. Transfer the salmon onto warmed plates, stir the chopped dill into the sauce and pour over the fish to serve.

Spanish mussels

Once washed and cleaned, mussels are one of the easiest foods to serve; they are ready in only a few minutes.

Serves 4

PREPARATION TIME
10 minutes

COOKING TIME
5–10 minutes

1.5kg (3lb 5oz) mussels

110g (4oz) chorizo

2 tbsp olive oil

120ml (4½fl oz) dry sherry or white wine

2 tbsp chopped parsley

4 lemon wedges, to serve

* Rinse the mussels in cold running water a couple of times to wash away any sand or grit. Give them a scrub to dislodge any barnacles or weed, then remove the 'beard' with a tug or a sharp knife. Discard any that are open and won't close when tapped against a surface.

* Cut the chorizo into 3mm (⅛in) slices. Pour the oil into a large saucepan on a medium heat and, when warm, add the chorizo. Cook for 1–2 minutes on each side or until the amber oils are released from the chorizo.

* Add the sherry, then the mussels, cover, and cook for 3–4 minutes or until all the mussels have opened. (Discard any that remain closed after cooking – don't eat these.)

* Stir in the parsley, then tip into wide, warmed bowls and serve with lemon wedges and toasted crusty white bread.

Very fast red prawn curry

Red curry paste is a useful ingredient to keep in your cupboard and is a great short cut for recreating that authentic Thai flavour.

Serves 4

PREPARATION TIME
10 minutes

COOKING TIME
5–10 minutes

2–4 tsp red curry paste

2 x 400ml tins of coconut milk

250g (9oz) raw, peeled tiger prawns or king prawns

1 tbsp chopped basil

2 tbsp fish sauce (nam pla)

* Place the curry paste in a large saucepan on a medium heat and cook for about 10 seconds. Pour in the coconut milk and bring to the boil, then tip in the prawns and simmer for 3–5 minutes or until they become opaque and are cooked through.

* Add the chopped basil and season with the fish sauce to taste. You can add some extra curry paste if you like it a little hotter. Serve immediately with boiled rice (see page 332) or noodles.

Yoghurt masala fish

The spiced yoghurt in this dish has several advantages. The complex aromas of garam masala marry well with a meaty white fish like haddock, red snapper or mullet, while the yoghurt ensures the meat stays perfectly moist and doesn't dry out under the grill. It also crisps up slightly in the heat, providing a welcome contrast in texture with the juicy fish.

Serves 6–8

PREPARATION TIME
15 minutes, plus marinating

COOKING TIME
25–30 minutes

1 x 1kg (2lb 3oz) whole fish such as haddock, red snapper or mullet (ask your fishmonger to gut and descale the fish)

½ tsp salt

2 tbsp sunflower oil

For the spiced yoghurt

3 tsp garam masala (to make your own, see page 129)

¼ tsp salt

Good squeeze of lemon juice

4–5 garlic cloves, peeled and crushed or finely grated

1 tbsp peeled and finely grated root ginger

100ml (3½fl oz) natural yoghurt

* Place the fish in a roasting tin and, using a long sharp knife, cut several quite deep slits, each about 2cm (¾in) apart, across the width of the fish on both sides. Rub the salt into these cuts and set aside for 10 minutes.

* Place all the ingredients for the spiced yoghurt in a bowl and stir to mix, then use all but about 2 tablespoons of this mixture to rub into both sides of the fish, and leave to marinate for 10 minutes.

* Preheat the grill to high.

* Drizzle half the sunflower oil over one side of the fish and place under the grill for about 10 minutes or until the yoghurt paste has started to brown. Turn the fish over, spread over the remaining paste and drizzle over the sunflower oil, then place under the grill for 15–20 minutes or until the yoghurt coating is lightly browned and the fish is opaque and cooked all the way through.

Sesame-crusted chicken

This is a quick way of adding crunch and flavour to a simple chicken breast. Fried Kale with Oyster Sauce (see the variation on page 319) makes an ideal accompaniment, the oyster sauce adding a similarly Oriental touch.

Serves 4

PREPARATION TIME
5 minutes

COOKING TIME
25–30 minutes

100g (3½oz) fresh white breadcrumbs

5 tbsp sesame seeds

3 tsp Chinese five-spice powder

Salt and freshly ground black pepper

4 skinless, boneless chicken breasts or 6 skinless, boneless thighs

2 eggs, beaten

4–6 tbsp sunflower oil

* Preheat the oven to 200°C (400°F), Gas mark 6.

* In a bowl, mix together the breadcrumbs, sesame seeds and Chinese five-spice powder. Season with salt and pepper and spread out on a plate.

* Dip the chicken in the beaten eggs, then roll in the breadcrumb mixture. Place on a baking tray and drizzle each breast or thigh with a tablespoon of sunflower oil. Place in the oven and bake for 25–30 minutes or until the sesame crust is golden and the chicken is cooked through. Serve with Kale with Oyster Sauce (see page 319) and boiled rice (see page 332) or noodles.

Chicken livers with onions

For those of us who love chicken livers, I can think of no better way of eating them than prepared in this way; still a little pink inside and combined with a rich onion gravy. If you have time, make some mash to go with them (see page 314), otherwise make sure to mop up every last drop with some good crusty bread.

Serves 2

PREPARATION TIME
5 minutes

COOKING TIME
30 minutes

40g (1½oz) butter

2 onions, peeled and thinly sliced

300g (11oz) chicken livers

Salt and freshly ground black pepper

25ml (1fl oz) dry sherry

100ml (3½fl oz) chicken or vegetable stock

* Melt half the butter in a frying pan on a medium–high heat and, when foaming, add the onions. Fry, stirring occasionally, for 15–20 minutes or until the onions are completely soft and golden. Tip the onions onto a plate and set aside.

* Season the chicken livers with salt and pepper, add the remaining butter to the pan and when it has melted and is starting to foam, add the chicken livers. Cook for 2–4 minutes on each side – they should be browned on the outside but still a little pink in the middle.

* Add the sherry, allowing it to bubble for 30 seconds, then add the cooked onions and stock. Stir together, bring to the boil, then reduce the heat and cook for 1–2 minutes or until the stock has slightly reduced. Serve immediately.

Chicken, parsnip and potato bake

Chicken thighs and drumsticks are so easy to cook. Mixed with onion and root vegetables and tossed in a little oil, they will be moist and juicy after baking in the oven, with a gorgeous golden skin. The garlic cloves are left unpeeled, their cooked flesh becoming a sweet and sticky paste that demands to be squeezed out and spread all over the crispy chicken.

Serves 4

PREPARATION TIME
10 minutes

COOKING TIME
45 minutes–1 hour

4 chicken drumsticks or thighs (with the skin left on)

2 red onions, peeled and cut through the root into 6 wedges

4 small floury potatoes, peeled and cut into 2–3cm (¾–1¼in) cubes

2 parsnips, peeled (and remove the woody core if the parsnips are particularly large) and cut into 4cm (1½in) pieces

12 cloves of garlic (unpeeled)

100ml (3½fl oz) olive oil

Salt and freshly ground black pepper

* Preheat the oven to 220°C (425°F), Gas mark 7.

* In a large bowl, mix together all the ingredients and season with salt and pepper.

* Spread out on a baking tray, season the chicken pieces with a little extra salt and pepper and place in the oven. Bake in the oven for 45 minutes to 1 hour or until the chicken is cooked through and the vegetables are golden and crispy.

Tarragon chicken

Tarragon and chicken are a classic combination. All the other ingredients are here simply to enhance this lovely marriage of flavours.

Serves 4

PREPARATION TIME
1 minute

COOKING TIME
15 minutes

25g (1oz) butter

4 chicken breasts

Salt and freshly ground black pepper

600ml (1 pint) chicken stock

6 tbsp crème fraîche

4 tbsp chopped tarragon

* Melt the butter in a frying pan on a high heat and, when foaming, add the chicken breasts. Season with salt and pepper and cook for 2–3 minutes on each side or until well browned, then stir in the remaining ingredients.

* Mix together well, scraping the bottom of the pan with a wooden spoon to dislodge any browned pieces and stir them into the sauce. Bring to the boil, then reduce the heat and simmer for 8 minutes or until the sauce has reduced and thickened and the chicken is opaque all the way through. Taste for seasoning and serve with boiled new potatoes.

Spiced fried chicken

I know it's not the healthiest way of cooking it, but sometimes I crave fried chicken and only the gorgeous crispness provided by deep-frying will do. The spiced flour not only makes a wonderfully crunchy crust, it also protects the chicken from the full heat of the oil, allowing the meat to stay perfectly moist and tender.

Serves 2–4

PREPARATION TIME
10 minutes

COOKING TIME
10 minutes

Vegetable oil, for deep-frying

1 tsp cumin seeds

75g (3oz) self-raising flour

1 tsp salt

1½ tsp caster sugar

1 tsp smoked paprika (optional)

200ml (7fl oz) milk

4 chicken legs or thighs (with the skin left on)

* Heat the vegetable oil in a deep-fat fryer to 160°C (325°F). Alternatively, pour the oil into a large saucepan to a depth of 2cm (¾in) and bring to the same temperature on the hob (checking with a sugar thermometer, or see tip below).

* To toast the cumin seeds, place them in a small frying pan on a high heat and cook, tossing frequently, for about 1 minute or until they are browned.

* Grind the cumin seeds into a powder with a pestle and mortar or place in a plastic bag and use a rolling pin to crush them. Then mix together in a bowl with the flour, salt, sugar and paprika (if using). Pour the milk into another bowl.

* Once the oil is hot, toss a piece of chicken in the milk, then roll in the spiced flour. Shake off any excess flour, then return to the milk and roll once again in the flour, patting it in place to make sure it stays stuck to the skin.

* Lower the chicken into the hot oil using a slotted spoon, then repeat with the remaining pieces. Deep-fry in batches if necessary. Each piece takes about 10 minutes and they are done when cooked through and a rich golden brown colour. When finished, remove from the oil and drain on kitchen paper. Serve with chips and the Red Cabbage Coleslaw (see page 323).

Rachel's tip

An easy way to check if cooking oil is hot enough for deep-frying is to drop in a cube of bread. If it comes back up to the top relatively quickly, the oil is the perfect temperature. If it immediately burns, the oil is too hot.

Rack of lamb

Rack of lamb must be the easiest cut of meat to cook and serve, as there's no tricky carving in front of your guests – you simply cut off two or three chops per person. Do make sure your butcher trims the rack first, however.

Serves 4–6

PREPARATION TIME
5 minutes

COOKING TIME
**30–40 minutes,
plus resting**

2 racks of lamb (about
1kg/2lb 3oz each),
trimmed

4 tbsp chopped rosemary
leaves

2 tbsp Dijon mustard

2 tbsp olive oil

2 cloves of garlic, peeled
and crushed or finely
grated

Salt and freshly ground
black pepper

400ml (14fl oz) chicken or
lamb stock

* Preheat the oven to 220°C (425°F), Gas mark 7.

* Remove the papery skin from each rack of lamb if they are still attached, then score the fat in a criss-cross pattern, spacing the lines 1–2cm (½–¾in) apart and trying not to cut into the meat.

* In a bowl, mix together the rosemary, mustard, olive oil and garlic. Rub the lamb all over with this mixture, then season with salt and pepper. Place in a roasting tin and roast in the oven for 25–35 minutes, depending on the weight of the lamb and how pink you like it to be.

* Remove from the oven and allow the meat to rest for 10 minutes before serving. To make the gravy, pour any fat out of the roasting tin, then add the stock to the tin and stir over a low–medium heat for 3–5 minutes to deglaze. Use a whisk to scrape the browned pieces from the bottom of the tin so they dissolve. Season with salt and pepper to taste.

* To serve, cut between the chops and give each person 2–3 chops and a generous serving of gravy. Serve with a variety of vegetables, such as Roasted New Potatoes and Green Beans with Anchovies and Toasted Almonds (see pages 313 and 327).

Sumac lamb chops

Sumac is a Middle Eastern berry that is crushed up and sold as a red spice powder. The flavour is quite distinctive, delivering a uniquely sour taste. You can get hold of sumac in specialist food shops and some big supermarkets.

Serves 4

PREPARATION TIME
5 minutes

COOKING TIME
4–8 minutes

3 tbsp olive oil

8 lamb chops

Salt and freshly ground black pepper

4 tsp sumac, plus extra to serve

2 tomatoes, cut into 1cm (½in) dice

300g (11oz) cucumber, cut into 1cm (½in) dice

150ml (5fl oz) natural yoghurt

* Place a large griddle pan or frying pan on a high heat and allow it to get quite hot. As the pan heats up, drizzle 1 teaspoon of olive oil over both sides of each chop, then season both sides with salt and pepper and sprinkle with 1 teaspoon of sumac, rubbing in the spice and seasoning with your fingers. Place in the hot pan and fry for 2–4 minutes on each side, depending on the thickness of the chops and how pink you like them.

* As the lamb chops cook, mix together the remaining ingredients in a bowl and season with salt and pepper. Divide the lamb chops and salad between plates and sprinkle each plate with a pinch of sumac.

Honey mustard pork chops

As meat is fried, it leaves behind little sticky brown nuggets in the bottom of the pan. Dissolving (or 'deglazing') these in the pan makes a sauce that is rich with the taste of the meat. This recipe includes the classic combination of honey for sweetness and Dijon mustard for a bit of a kick. The cream is essential for bringing everything together.

Serves 4

PREPARATION TIME
2 minutes

COOKING TIME
10–15 minutes

2 tbsp olive oil

4 pork chops

Salt and freshly ground black pepper

4 tbsp runny honey

4 tbsp single or regular cream

2 tbsp Dijon mustard

* Pour the olive oil into a frying pan on a medium heat. Season the pork chops with salt and pepper and, when the oil is hot, add them to the pan and fry for 3–5 minutes on each side or until just white all the way through. (Try not to overcook the chops, however, or the meat will taste tough.)

* Meanwhile, place the honey in a bowl with the cream and mustard and mix together. When the pork chops are cooked, transfer them to warmed plates.

* Add the honey mixture to the frying pan, then bring to the boil, reduce the heat and allow the sauce to bubble for 20–30 seconds or until the liquid has thickened and become treacle-like in colour. As the sauce heats, use a wooden spoon to scrape the sticky pork bits from the bottom of the pan so that they dissolve in the liquid. Season with a little salt and pepper, then pour over the pork chops and serve.

Fried potatoes with cabbage and chorizo

An unashamedly rustic dish, this is perfect for eating on a cold winter's day.

Serves 4

PREPARATION TIME
15 minutes

COOKING TIME
20–25 minutes

2 tbsp olive oil

375g (13oz) chorizo, cut into 1cm (½in) thick slices

625g (1lb 6oz) floury potatoes, peeled and cut into 2cm (¾in) chunks

2 onions, peeled and sliced

4 large cloves of garlic, peeled and crushed or finely grated

Salt and freshly ground black pepper

1 Savoy cabbage, quartered, core removed and leaves shredded crossways (225g/8oz prepared weight)

* Pour the olive oil into a large, wide saucepan or frying pan on a low–medium heat and, when warm, add the chorizo and cook for a few minutes on both sides for 2–3 minutes on each side or until golden. By this stage the deep orange oils will have been released by the chorizo. Remove the chorizo, leaving the oil in the pan, and set aside.

* Add the potatoes, onions and garlic to the pan and season with salt and pepper. Increase the heat to medium–high and cook for 10–15 minutes, stirring regularly and scraping the bottom of the pan to release the delicious caramelised bits and mix them in.

* Once the onions are golden and the potatoes very nearly cooked, add 50ml (2fl oz) water, followed by the shredded cabbage and the cooked chorizo, and toss in the pan for 2–3 minutes or until the cabbage is wilted. Taste for seasoning and serve.

Flavoured butters for steak

Each recipe serves 4

PREPARATION TIME
5 minutes, plus chilling

These butters are so useful, giving instant additional flavour to steak, chicken, pork, lamb or fish. Keep in the fridge for a week.

Tarragon mustard butter

5g (3oz) butter, softened

2 cloves of garlic, crushed or finely grated

3 tsp Dijon mustard

2 tsp chopped tarragon

6 black peppercorns, lightly crushed

Salt

* In a bowl, mix together all the ingredients, seasoning with salt to taste. Place on a piece of baking parchment or cling film and use this to help roll the flavoured butter into a log about 2.5cm (1in) in diameter. Transfer to the fridge and keep chilled until needed, then cut into slices about 1cm (½ in) thick to serve.

Red wine butter

COOKING TIME
10–15 minutes

150ml (5fl oz) red wine

3 cloves of garlic, peeled and finely chopped

75g (3oz) butter, softened

2 tsp chopped thyme

6 peppercorns, crushed

Salt

* Pour the wine into a small saucepan on a high heat and add the garlic. Bring to the boil and allow to bubble and reduce until roughly 1 tablespoon of liquid remains in the pan, then remove from the heat and leave to cool. When the wine mixture has cooled, pour it into a bowl, add the butter, thyme, pepper and a little salt and mix together well. Taste for seasoning, then place on a piece of baking parchment or cling film and roll into a log, chilling in the fridge until needed (see Tarragon Mustard Butter, above).

Orange chilli butter

75g (3oz) butter, softened

Grated zest of ½ orange

¼–½ red chilli, deseeded and finely chopped

1 tsp peeled and finely grated root ginger

6 peppercorns, crushed

Salt

* In a bowl, mix together all the ingredients, seasoning with salt to taste. Place on a piece of baking parchment or cling film and roll into a log, chilling in the fridge until needed (see Tarragon Mustard Butter, above).

Apple fool

Fruit fools are a very old type of pudding, dating back some 500 years. I used to imagine the dish was so called because any fool could make it, but the word is believed to derive from the French verb *fouler*, meaning to crush or press. Whatever the case, it is so easy that any fool can indeed make it!

Serves 4–6 (v)

PREPARATION TIME
10 minutes

COOKING TIME
5–10 minutes

2 cooking apples (about 550g/1lb 3oz in total), peeled, cored and cut into 2–3cm (¾–1¼in) chunks

100g (3½oz) caster sugar

250ml (9fl oz) double or regular cream

4–6 glasses or bowls

* Place the apple in a small saucepan with the sugar and 100ml (3½ fl oz) water and set on a low–medium heat. Cook for 5–10 minutes or until soft, then stir with a spoon to purée them. Set aside to cool completely.

* Meanwhile, pour the cream into a bowl and whip into stiff peaks, then store in the fridge until the apple mixture has fully cooled.

* Fold the apple purée into the whipped cream and serve straightaway or cover with cling film or a plate and store in the fridge for up to 24 hours. When you are ready to serve, pour into the glasses or bowls and serve with Shortbread Biscuits (see page 341).

Hot buttered plum pudding

The texture of these plums is fantastic as the sugar caramelises, forming a crunchy crust to contrast with the rich red juicy plums.

Serves 4 (v)

PREPARATION TIME
10 minutes

COOKING TIME
35 minutes

4 slices of white bread

50g (2oz) butter, softened

4 plums, stones removed and flesh cut into 5mm (¼in) thick slices

75g (3oz) caster sugar

* Preheat the oven to 220°C (425°F), Gas mark 7.

* Remove the crusts from the bread and butter generously on one side. Place, butter side down, in an ovenproof dish in which all the bread will fit in one layer. Use the remaining butter to spread over the bread, then cover with the plum slices and sprinkle with the sugar.

* Place in the oven and bake for 35 minutes or until the plums are cooked and slightly caramelised at the edges. Serve immediately with cream or ice cream, if you wish.

Lemon posset

In this timeless dessert, the cream thickens as it boils with the sugar, while the lemon juice adds just a touch of sharpness.

Serves 6 (v)

PREPARATION TIME
2 minutes

COOKING TIME
5 minutes, plus cooling

400ml (14fl oz) double or regular cream

150g (5oz) caster or granulated sugar

50ml (2fl oz) lemon juice

Six 100ml (3½fl oz) ramekins, cups or glasses

* Pour the cream into a small saucepan on a medium heat, add the sugar and bring to the boil, stirring to dissolve the sugar. Reduce the heat and simmer for 5 minutes, taking care not to let the cream boil over.

* Remove the pan from the heat and stir in the lemon juice. Allow to cool for about 15 minutes, then divide between the ramekins, cups or glasses. Chill in the fridge for a couple of hours or until set, then serve on their own or with Shortbread Biscuits (see page 341) and a little whipped cream.

Cardamom and orange semifreddo

This frozen dessert is very similar to ice cream (semifreddo means 'half cold' in Italian) but it's a thousand times easier to make. Heating the cream with the ground cardamom infuses it with the flavour and exotic aroma of the spice.

Serves 6 (v)

PREPARATION TIME
15 minutes

COOKING TIME
2 minutes, plus freezing

15 green cardamom pods

225ml (8fl oz) double or regular cream

3 egg whites

100g (3½oz) caster sugar

Finely grated zest of 1 orange

13 x 23cm (5 x 9in) loaf tin

* Line the loaf tin with a double layer of cling film, leaving enough excess to fold over the finished mixture to cover.

* Place the cardamom pods on a chopping board, lay the flat side of a large knife over the top and press down to lightly crush. Remove the seeds (discarding the pods) and grind to a powder with a pestle and mortar or place in a plastic bag and use a rolling pin to crush them.

* Pour 50ml (2fl oz) of the cream into a saucepan and add the crushed cardamom seeds. Bring to the boil, then reduce the heat and simmer for 2 minutes. Remove from the heat and allow to stand for about 5 minutes or until cool.

* Place the egg whites in a large, spotlessly clean bowl or in an electric food mixer and whisk in the mixer, or using a hand-held electric beater, until they form soft peaks. With the machine still running, gradually pour in the caster sugar and keep whisking for about 5 minutes or until the meringue mixture forms stiff glossy peaks.

* In a separate bowl, whip the remaining cream until it forms soft peaks. Fold in the cooled cardamom cream, then add the orange zest and stir in until everything is evenly distributed.

* Carefully fold the egg whites into the cream until completely combined. Fill the prepared loaf tin with the mixture, folding over the excess cling film to cover. Place in the freezer for about 6 hours or overnight. To serve, carefully lift from the tin, peel away the cling film and cut into slices.

Yoghurt, apricot and pistachio pots

These yoghurt pots have a taste of the Middle East, and though they're deliciously sweet, they also manage to tick the healthy box. A lovely light dessert, they're also perfect for breakfast.

Serves 4 (v)

PREPARATION TIME
10 minutes

COOKING TIME
10 minutes, plus cooling

250g (9oz) dried apricots, halved

200ml (7fl oz) freshly squeezed orange juice

6 tsp runny honey

150ml (5fl oz) natural Greek yoghurt

15g (½oz) shelled pistachios, roughly chopped

four glasses

* Place the apricots in a small saucepan with the orange juice and 2 teaspoons of the honey. Simmer for about 10 minutes or until soft and plump, then remove from the heat and allow to cool.

* Divide the fruit and its juices between the glasses, then add the yoghurt, spooning it over the top of the fruit before drizzling each serving with 1 teaspoon of honey and scattering over the chopped pistachios.

Chocolate zabaglione

The classic Italian dessert zabaglione is ancient, thought to date back a thousand years. The dish is traditionally flavoured with Marsala, a sweet white wine, but you can also use a sweet sherry. The addition of chocolate to the basic recipe gives it a luxuriantly silky-soft texture.

Serves 4 (v)

PREPARATION TIME
5 minutes

COOKING TIME
10 minutes

25ml (1fl oz) whipping, double or regular cream

50g (2oz) dark chocolate, broken into pieces, or dark chocolate drops

4 egg yolks

75g (3oz) caster sugar

50ml (2fl oz) Marsala or sweet sherry

Pinch of salt

four glasses

* Pour the cream into a saucepan and bring to the boil, then remove from the heat, add the chocolate and stir until melted. Set aside somewhere warm.

* In a heatproof bowl, whisk together the egg yolks with the sugar, sherry or Marsala and salt until well mixed. Place the bowl over a saucepan of simmering water and, using an electric hand-held beater set on a medium speed, beat the mixture for 4–5 minutes or until it is thick and creamy (see tip below).

* Remove from the heat and fold in the melted chocolate, then divide between the serving glasses and serve with fresh strawberries or raspberries, Shortbread Biscuits (see page 341) or both.

Rachel's tip

To check that the mixture is at the right stage, lift out the beater and, with the mixture that drops from the whisk attachments, make a figure of eight in the mixture below. If the mixture is thick enough, you should still be able to read the 'eight' by the time you've finished writing it.

Rhubarb and ginger meringues

By balancing rhubarb's inherent sharpness with the sweetness of sugar, its intense flavour comes through all the more. Rhubarb and ginger are a fantastic combination and this fruit fool looks impressive served in the middle of the meringues, though if you prefer you can serve the fool in bowls or glasses.

Serves 4 (v)

PREPARATION TIME
15 minutes

COOKING TIME
10–15 minutes, plus cooling

2 large egg whites

125g (4½oz) caster sugar

For the rhubarb and ginger fool

175g (6oz) trimmed rhubarb, cut into 1cm (½in) lengths

75g (3oz) caster sugar

1 tsp peeled and grated root ginger

125ml (4½fl oz) whipping, double or regular cream, softly whipped

* Preheat the oven to 160°C (325°F), Gas mark 3. Line a baking sheet with baking parchment.

* Place the egg whites in a large, spotlessly clean bowl or in an electric food mixer and whisk in the mixer, or using a hand-held electric beater, until they form soft peaks. With the machine still running, gradually pour in the caster sugar and keep whisking for about 5 minutes or until the meringue mixture forms stiff glossy peaks.

* Spoon 4 large blobs of meringue onto the baking sheet, spaced well apart. Using the back of your spoon, spread each blob into a round about 8cm (3in) in diameter, then use the spoon to make a well in the centre (in which the rhubarb fool will sit).

* Place in the oven and bake for 10–15 minutes or until crisp on the outside but still marshmallowy in the middle. To check that they're done, carefully lift one off the paper: if it comes away cleanly, it's ready. Remove from the oven and place on a wire rack to cool. (Don't worry if they crack a bit around the edges – it's part of their charm.)

* To make the rhubarb fool, place the rhubarb, sugar and ginger in a saucepan with 25ml (1fl oz) water and cook, uncovered, on a medium heat for 4–5 minutes or until the rhubarb is stewed to a mush and the syrup is thick. Allow to cool, then fold into the whipped cream.

* Place the meringues on a plate, spoon a lovely big dollop of fool over the top of each and serve.

Chocolate mousse cake

This cake has to be made to be believed. It is so simple to throw together yet tastes and looks like you slaved over it for hours.

Serves 8 (v)

PREPARATION TIME
15 minutes

COOKING TIME
25–30 minutes,
plus cooling

300g (11oz) dark
chocolate, broken
into pieces, or dark
chocolate drops

150g (5oz) butter

5 eggs

50g (2oz) caster sugar

Cocoa powder, for
dusting

*20cm (8in) diameter
spring-form/loose-
bottomed cake tin*

* Preheat the oven to 180°C (350°F), Gas mark 4. Line the base of the cake tin with a disc of baking parchment and grease the sides with butter.

* Place the chocolate and butter in a heatproof bowl set over a saucepan of simmering water and allow to melt, then remove from the heat and set aside.

* Place the eggs and sugar in a separate bowl and, using a hand-held electric beater or electric mixer, whisk for 7–10 minutes or until the mixture forms a light, pale mousse.

* Fold the chocolate mixture into the eggs until fully combined, then pour into the prepared tin and bake for 20–22 minutes or until the cake is almost set. Allow to cool down completely in the tin before removing, then dust with cocoa powder and cut into slices to serve.

Strawberry and nectarine tart

In summertime, I always make the most of strawberries, adding them to pavlovas, or using them to flavour ice cream. They are also delicious simply drizzled with a few drops of good-quality balsamic vinegar or partnered with nectarines or peaches, as in this recipe. This tart works so well using this sunny combination.

Serves 6–8 (v)

PREPARATION TIME
10 minutes

COOKING TIME
20–25 minutes

200g (7oz) strawberries, hulled and sliced

5 small–medium nectarines (about 400g/14oz in total), stones removed and flesh cut into 5mm (¼in) thick slices

1 tbsp lemon juice

1–2 tbsp caster sugar

500g (1lb 2oz) ready-rolled puff pastry (or roll out a block of puff pastry to a thickness of about 4mm/⅛in)

* Preheat the oven to 220°C (425°F), Gas mark 7.

* Place the strawberries and nectarines in a bowl and mix together with the lemon juice and caster sugar (adding more or less sugar depending on how sweet the fruit is).

* Trim the pastry into a 25 x 30cm (10 x 12in) rectangle and transfer to a baking sheet. Carefully arrange the strawberries and nectarines in overlapping alternate slices on top of the pastry, leaving a 1cm (½in) border all the way round.

* Place in the oven and bake for 20–25 minutes or until the pastry has turned golden and the fruit is bubbling and slightly caramelised. Serve immediately, perhaps with a little mascarpone.

Pear and cinnamon tart

This tart takes only minutes to prepare. If you can only get block puff pastry, roll it to a thickness of about 4mm (⅛in).

Serves 6–8 (v)

PREPARATION TIME
10 minutes

COOKING TIME
25–30 minutes

4 pears

100g (3½oz) caster sugar

½ tbsp ground cinnamon

25g (1oz) butter, melted

500g (1lb 2oz) ready-rolled puff pastry (or see introduction, above)

* Preheat the oven to 220°C (425°F), Gas mark 7.

* Leaving the skin on, core and cut the pears into 5mm (¼ in) thick slices. Put in a bowl and mix with the sugar, cinnamon and butter. Trim the pastry into a 25–30cm (10–12in) rectangle and transfer to a baking sheet.

* Arrange the pear slices, slightly overlapping in rows, on the pastry, leaving a 1cm (½ in) border all the way round.

* Bake for 25–30 minutes or until the pastry is golden brown and the pears are slightly caramelised at the edges. Remove from the oven and serve the tart immediately, either on its own or with some vanilla ice cream or whipped cream.

Chocolate and banana tart

Using ready-rolled puff pastry, this tart is so quick to make. The topping is ideal for children's parties.

Serves 6–8 (v)

PREPARATION TIME
10 minutes

COOKING TIME
20–25 minutes

4 bananas, cut into 5mm (¼in) slices, at an angle

1 tbsp lemon juice

500g (1lb 2oz) ready-rolled puff pastry (or see the introduction above)

2–3 tbsp chocolate and hazelnut spread

2 tsp soft dark brown sugar

* Preheat the oven to 220°C (425°F), Gas mark 7.

* Place the banana slices in a bowl and mix with the lemon juice. Trim the pastry into a 25 x 30cm (10 x 12in) rectangle and transfer to a baking sheet.

* Next, spread the chocolate and hazelnut spread, not too thickly, on the pastry, leaving a 1cm (½ in) border all the way round. Arrange the banana slices on top in overlapping rows, then sprinkle over the sugar, taking care to distribute it evenly over the bananas.

* Place in the oven and bake for 20–25 minutes or until the bananas are cooked and the pastry is golden.

One Pot

Cooking a whole meal in one pot has a number of advantages. First, of course, the washing up is kept to an absolute minimum. Next, with many recipes, you can leave them to cook while you get on with your other favourite activities (or chores!) while your dinner cooks itself. With everything in one dish there is also no difficult coordination of side dishes that all have to be ready at once. But one of my favourite reasons is that since these often get a chance to simmer away slowly, the flavours are really given time to get to know one another.

Minestrone

There is no set recipe for this classic Italian soup. It is a dish that welcomes almost any vegetable in season with open arms.

2 tbsp olive oil

150g (5oz) bacon (in the piece or about 6 rashers), cut into 2cm (¾in) dice

1 onion, peeled and sliced

2 cloves of garlic, peeled and finely sliced

Salt and freshly ground black pepper

2 large tomatoes, chopped

100ml (3½fl oz) red wine

1.5 litres (2½ pints) chicken or vegetable stock

Pinch of granulated or caster sugar

1 x 400g tin of cannellini or flageolet beans, drained and rinsed

2 carrots, peeled and cut into 1cm (½in) dice

1 potato, peeled and cut into 1cm (½in) dice

1 stick of celery, trimmed and cut into 1cm (½in) dice

¼ small cabbage, such as Savoy, core removed and leaves shredded crossways

75g (3oz) dried spaghetti, broken into pieces

1 tsp chopped thyme leaves

2 tbsp chopped parsley

4 tbsp freshly grated Parmesan cheese, plus extra, to serve

Serves 4–6

PREPARATION TIME
20 minutes

COOKING TIME
50 minutes

* Pour half the olive oil into a large saucepan on a high heat and, when hot, add the bacon and fry for 4 minutes or until the fat has rendered and the bacon is golden. Reduce the heat to medium, add the remaining olive oil and stir in the onion and garlic. Season with salt (but not too much as the bacon is salty) and pepper and cook for 6–8 minutes or until the onion is soft but not browned.

* Add the chopped tomatoes, red wine and stock and season with salt (again, not too much) and a pinch of sugar. Bring to the boil, then reduce the heat to a simmer. Add the beans and carrots, bring back up to a simmer and cook for 15 minutes, then add the potato and cook for a further 10 minutes.

* Season with a little more salt, then add the celery, cabbage and spaghetti. Cook for 8–10 minutes or until the pasta is tender, then remove from the heat and stir in the herbs and Parmesan cheese.

* Taste for seasoning and serve with some more freshly grated Parmesan cheese scattered over the top.

Carrot, ginger and coconut soup

The slight spiciness of ginger combines well with the sweetness of the carrots, which are grated in this recipe so that they cook beautifully quickly.

Serves 8
(v, if using vegetable stock)

PREPARATION TIME
10 minutes

COOKING TIME
15–20 minutes

3 tbsp sunflower oil

2 onions, peeled and roughly chopped

2 cloves of garlic, peeled and finely chopped

800g (1¾lb) carrots, peeled and grated

2 tbsp peeled and finely chopped root ginger

(1 pint 9fl oz) chicken or vegetable stock

1 x 400ml tin of coconut milk

Salt and freshly ground black pepper

2 tbsp chopped coriander, to serve

* Pour the sunflower oil into a large saucepan on a medium heat and, when hot, add the onions and garlic. Cover with a lid and sweat for 6–8 minutes or until softened but not browned.

* Stir in the grated carrots with the ginger, then cover again with the lid and cook, stirring occasionally, for 8–10 minutes or until the vegetables have softened.

* Pour in the stock and coconut milk, bring to the boil, then reduce the heat and simmer for 2–3 minutes.

* Remove from the heat and liquidise the soup in a blender, or use a hand-held blender, then place back on the hob and heat through again. Season with salt and pepper and serve with a sprinkling of fresh coriander.

Red lentil soup

Lentils are substantial enough to turn a soup into a proper meal – a frugal and highly nutritious one at that.

Serves 4
(v, if using vegetable stock)

PREPARATION TIME
10 minutes

COOKING TIME
30–35 minutes

2 tbsp sunflower oil

1 onion, peeled and chopped

2 cloves of garlic, peeled and finely chopped

1 tomato, chopped

¼–½ red chilli, deseeded and chopped

1 tsp peeled and finely chopped root ginger

150g (5oz) red lentils

500ml (18fl oz) chicken or vegetable stock or water

2 tbsp chopped parsley

Salt and freshly ground black pepper

1 tbsp lemon juice

* Pour the sunflower oil into a large saucepan on a medium heat and, when hot, add the onion and garlic. Fry, stirring occasionally, for 6–8 minutes or until the onion is completely soft and a little golden.

* Stir in the tomato, chilli and ginger and cook for a further 5 minutes, then add the lentils and stock or water. (The lentils should be covered by about 1cm (½ in) of stock or water.) Bring to the boil, then reduce the heat and cook for 15–20 minutes or until the lentils are soft.

* Add the parsley, then remove from the heat and purée in a blender or use a hand-held blender. Return to the hob to reheat, seasoning with salt, pepper and lemon juice to serve.

Cauliflower soup

Cauliflower can be somewhat neglected as a vegetable, but it makes a delicious, delicately flavoured soup with a particularly lovely velvety texture.

Serves 6–8
(v, if using vegetable stock)

PREPARATION TIME
10 minutes

COOKING TIME
20 minutes

75g (3oz) butter

1 large onion, peeled and chopped

1 leek, trimmed and sliced

1 cauliflower, cut into florets

Salt and freshly ground black pepper

1–1.2 litres (1¾–2 pints) chicken or vegetable stock

To serve

60–75ml (2½–3fl oz) crème fraîche

2–3 tbsp lemon juice

1–2 tbsp chopped chives

* Melt the butter in a large saucepan, add the onion and leek, cover with a butter wrapper or piece of greaseproof paper and sweat on a low–medium heat, stirring occasionally, for 6–8 minutes or until the vegetables are soft but not browned.

* Stir in the cauliflower florets and continue to cook, stirring occasionally, for a further 5 minutes, then season with salt and pepper.

* Pour in 1 litre (1¾ pints) of the stock and bring to the boil, then allow to boil for a further 4–5 minutes or until the cauliflower is soft.

* Remove from the heat and liquidise until smooth in a blender or use a hand-held blender. Return to the hob to reheat, adding a little more stock if you would like a thinner soup. Taste for seasoning, then divide between bowls, serving with a spoonful of crème fraîche, a squeeze of lemon and a sprinkling of chives.

Smoked sausage, bean and root vegetable soup

Smoked sausage will flavour the whole broth in a soup or stew with a distinctive smoky taste. I've used cabanossi here, but you can use whatever smoked sausage you can find.

Serves 4–6

PREPARATION TIME
15 minutes

COOKING TIME
35–40 minutes

1 tbsp olive oil

150g (5oz) smoked sausage, such as cabanossi, sliced into 5mm (¼in) pieces

1 onion, peeled and chopped

4 cloves of garlic, peeled and finely chopped

Salt and freshly ground black pepper

1.5 litres (2½ pints) chicken or vegetable stock

1 bay leaf

2 sprigs of thyme

1 carrot, peeled and cut into 1cm (½in) dice

2 floury potatoes, peeled and cut into 1cm (½in) dice

1 parsnip, peeled (remove the woody core if the parsnips are particularly large) and cut into 1cm (½in) dice

1 x 400g tin of white beans such as cannellini or haricot, drained and rinsed

* Pour the olive oil into a large saucepan on a medium heat and, when hot, add the sausage pieces. Stir-fry for 1 minute and then add the onion and garlic. Season with salt and pepper, then cover with a lid and cook for 5 minutes or until the onion is soft but not browned.

* Add the stock, along with the bay leaf and thyme, and bring to the boil, then reduce the heat to a simmer. Season with salt and pepper, add the carrot and cook, uncovered, for 15 minutes.

* Tip the potatoes and parsnip into the pan, along with the cannellini or haricot beans, and cook for a further 15 minutes or until the vegetables are soft. Taste for seasoning, then divide between bowls to serve.

Asparagus and goat's cheese risotto

The asparagus and peas give this risotto an intense summery freshness. Baking the risotto in the oven, rather than cooking it on the hob in the conventional way, also makes it a wonderfully fuss-free dish. Choose firm green stalks of asparagus.

Serves 4

PREPARATION TIME
5 minutes

COOKING TIME
25–30 minutes

2 tbsp olive oil

1 onion, peeled and finely chopped

Salt and freshly ground black pepper

300g (11oz) risotto rice

100ml (3½fl oz) dry white wine

850ml (1½ pints) vegetable or chicken stock

10 asparagus spears

75g (3oz) peas (fresh or frozen)

25g (1oz) butter

50g (2oz) Parmesan cheese, finely grated

75g (3oz) soft goat's cheese

Large ovenproof saucepan with a lid

* Preheat the oven to 180°C (350°F), Gas mark 4.

* Pour the olive oil into the saucepan on a medium heat and, when hot, add the chopped onion. Season with salt and pepper, then reduce the heat to low, cover with a lid and cook for 6–8 minutes or until the onion is soft but not browned.

* Remove the lid and increase the heat to medium, stir in the rice and cook for 1 minute, then pour in the wine and bring to a simmer. Cook for 2 minutes or until the wine has evaporated, then pour in the stock, season again and bring to the boil. Cover with the lid and place in the oven to cook for 7 minutes.

* Meanwhile, prepare the asparagus. Snap off the woody ends, then cut off the top 3cm (1¼ in) of each spear at an angle and slice the rest of the stalk, also at an angle, into pieces about 1cm (½ in) long.

* Remove the risotto from the oven and stir in all of the asparagus, cover the pan again and cook for a further 7–9 minutes or until the rice is almost tender, then stir in the peas and return to the oven for just 2 more minutes.

* Once the rice and peas are cooked, beat in the butter and Parmesan cheese quite vigorously using a wooden spoon but without breaking up the asparagus pieces. Taste for seasoning, then serve on warmed plates with the goat's cheese crumbled over the top.

Kale and bean stew

I love the deep nourishment that a bean and vegetable stew can provide in winter. Leafy kale is a great winter vegetable and is full of nutrients. It's great to have something green on the table when there's so little green outside.

Serves 6–8
(v, if using vegetable stock)

PREPARATION TIME
10 minutes

COOKING TIME
40 minutes

3 tbsp olive oil

1 carrot, peeled and chopped

1 stick of celery, trimmed and chopped

4 shallots, peeled and chopped

2 cloves of garlic, peeled and finely chopped

Salt and freshly ground black pepper

250ml (9fl oz) dry white wine

2 x 400g tins of white beans, such as cannellini, butter, or haricot, drained and rinsed

800ml–1 litre (1 pint 9fl oz–1¾ pints) chicken or vegetable stock

3 sprigs of thyme

1 bay leaf

500g (1lb 2oz) (prepared weight) kale leaves, stalks and centre ribs removed and leaves shredded

1 tbsp sherry vinegar

2 tbsp parsley, to serve

* Pour the olive oil into a large saucepan on a medium heat and, when hot, add the carrot, celery, shallots and garlic. Season with salt and pepper, then cook, stirring occasionally, for 10–12 minutes or until completely soft and lightly browned.

* Add the white wine, bring to a simmer and cook for about 5 minutes or until the liquid is slightly reduced. Add the beans, 800ml (1 pint 9fl oz) of the stock and the thyme and bay leaf. Bring to the boil, then reduce the heat to low and simmer for about 15 minutes.

* Add the kale and allow the stew to simmer for a further 3–5 minutes or until the kale is tender, then remove the thyme and bay leaf. If you would like a thinner stew, add a little more stock at this stage. Stir in the sherry vinegar, then taste for seasoning and serve in bowls with a sprinkling of parsley.

Mediterranean pasta

This simple one-pot pasta dish has all the flavours of the Mediterranean. The caramelising of the onions at the start brings out a lovely sweetness in the tomatoes, while the other ingredients add delicious contrasts in taste and texture.

Serves 4
(v, if using vegetable stock)

PREPARATION TIME
15 minutes

COOKING TIME
30–35 minutes

15g (½oz) butter

3 tbsp olive oil

1 onion, peeled and finely sliced

2 cloves of garlic, peeled and sliced

1 large red pepper, deseeded and cut into 5mm (¼in) thick slices

200g (7oz) chorizo, cut into 7mm (⅜in) thick slices

1 x 400g tin of tomatoes, chopped

600ml (1 pint) chicken or vegetable stock

1 tsp caster sugar

350g (12oz) dried pasta, such as fusilli, penne or conchiglie

Salt and freshly ground black pepper

125g (4½oz) mozzarella, grated

50g (2oz) olives, pitted and chopped

2 tbsp torn basil leaves

* Place the butter and olive oil in a large saucepan on a medium heat. When the butter has melted and starts to foam, add the onion and garlic and cook for 10–15 minutes, stirring regularly, until the onion is soft and a little caramelised.

* Add the sliced pepper and chorizo and cook for a further 3 minutes, then pour in the tomatoes and all their juice, along with the stock, sugar, pasta and ½ teaspoon of salt. Bring to the boil, then reduce the heat to low, cover with a lid and cook for 10–12 minutes or until the pasta is just tender.

* Remove from the heat, stir in the mozzarella, olives and basil, add a grinding of black pepper and then divide between bowls to serve.

Fish stew

This is a lovely light fish stew that just cries out for crusty white bread to mop up all the delicious juices. Use whatever seafood is at its freshest – a combination of contrasting tastes and textures is what you're aiming for.

Serves 4–6

PREPARATION TIME
15 minutes

COOKING TIME
20 minutes

450g (1lb) mussels

4 large tomatoes

4 tbsp olive oil

200g (7oz) leeks, trimmed and cut into 7mm (⅜in) thick slices

1 red pepper, deseeded and cut into 1–2cm (½–¾in) dice

Salt and freshly ground black pepper

300ml (½ pint) chicken or fish stock

Good pinch of granulated or caster sugar

12 raw, peeled prawns, langoustines or tiger prawns (about 225g/8oz in total)

300g (11oz) skinless white fish fillets, such as cod or haddock, cut into 2cm (¾in) chunks

2 tbsp chopped parsley, to serve

* First prepare the mussels. Rinse the shells in cold running water a couple of times to wash away any sand or grit. Give them a scrub to dislodge any barnacles or bits of weed, then remove the 'beard' with a tug or a sharp knife. Discard any that are open and won't close when tapped against a hard surface.

* Next, peel the tomatoes by scoring a cross at the top of each tomato with a sharp knife, then placing in a bowl and covering with boiling water. Leave in the water for 15–20 seconds, then drain, rinse in cold water and peel the skin from each tomato. Chop the peeled tomatoes into small pieces and set aside.

* Pour the olive oil into a large saucepan on a medium heat, add the leeks and red pepper and season with salt and pepper. Cook for 4 minutes or until a little softened, then add the chopped tomatoes, stock and sugar. Bring to the boil, then reduce the heat, cover with a lid and cook for a further 7–8 minutes or until the tomatoes are soft.

* Tip in the mussels, prawns and fish, bring back up to the boil, then reduce the heat, cover with the lid and simmer gently for 2–3 minutes or until the fish and seafood are cooked. (The fish and prawns should be opaque and the mussels opened – discard any that remain closed.) Season to taste, sprinkle over the parsley and serve with chunks of crusty bread.

Fish chowder

Seafood chowder is the quintessential comfort food in a bowl. I love its creamy richness and always make it using some smoked fish. You can also add some whole mussels in their shells (be sure to discard any that remain closed after cooking).

Serves 4

PREPARATION TIME
10 minutes

COOKING TIME
15–20 minutes

Olive oil

100g (3½oz) streaky bacon (in the piece or about 3 rashers), cut into 1cm (½in) dice

1 small onion, peeled and chopped

Salt and freshly ground black pepper

175g (6oz) potatoes, peeled and cut into 1cm (½in) cubes

500ml (18fl oz) chicken stock

350ml (12fl oz) milk

Pinch of cayenne pepper

200g (7oz) fish fillets, a mixture of salmon and a white fish such as pollock, haddock or cod, cut into 2–3cm (¾–1¼in) chunks

100g (3½oz) smoked haddock or smoked salmon, cut into 2cm (¾in) pieces

1 tbsp chopped chives

1 tbsp chopped parsley

* Pour a small drizzle of olive oil into a large saucepan on a medium heat and, when hot, tip in the bacon. Fry for 4–5 minutes, stirring occasionally, until all the fat has rendered and the bacon is crispy and golden brown.

* Add the onion, season with salt and pepper (bearing in mind that the bacon is quite salty) and cook for another 4–5 minutes, then add the potatoes with the stock and milk and cayenne pepper.

* Bring to the boil, then reduce the heat and simmer for 3 minutes or until the cubes of potato are half cooked. Add the fish and gently simmer for another 3–4 minutes or until the fish is opaque and the potatoes are tender. Season with salt and pepper to taste and stir in the chopped herbs to serve.

Easy paella

The size of paella pans in Spanish markets can be amazing, with some measuring a metre or more across. Thankfully all that's necessary to make paella at home is a relatively wide frying pan.

Serves 4–6

PREPARATION TIME
10 minutes

COOKING TIME
35 minutes

125g (4½oz) raw, peeled prawns or a mixture of prawns and skinless white fish fillets, such as pollock, haddock, cod or hake

4 tbsp olive oil

1 onion, peeled and finely chopped

2 cloves of garlic, peeled and finely chopped

Salt and freshly ground black pepper

300g (11oz) paella rice

200ml (7fl oz) white wine

Good pinch of saffron

1 red pepper, deseeded and cut into 5mm (¼in) thick slices

250g (9oz) pork fillet, cut into 2cm (¾in) cubes

550ml (19fl oz) chicken stock

75g (3oz) peas (fresh or frozen)

Juice of ½ lemon

25cm (10in) diameter paella pan or heavy-based frying pan with a lid

* Cut the prawns in half lengthways and the fish (if using) into 2cm (¾in) chunks.

* Pour the olive oil into the paella pan or frying pan on a medium heat. When the oil is hot, add the onion and garlic, season with salt and pepper and cook for 7–8 minutes or until softened and a little golden.

* Turn up the heat and stir in the rice, allowing it to toast for a minute in the pan before adding the wine and saffron. Bring to the boil, then reduce the heat and allow the liquid to bubble for 3–4 minutes or until the wine has evaporated.

* At this point, place the red pepper and pork in the pan and toss on the heat for a couple of minutes or until the pork has lost almost all of its raw pink colour on the outside.

* Pour in the stock and bring back up to the boil, then turn the heat down to low and simmer, uncovered, for about 15 minutes, stirring occasionally, until the rice is just about cooked.

* Tip in the prawns and fish (if using), together with the peas, put a lid on the pan and cook for 2–3 minutes or until the seafood is opaque and peas are tender. (If the mixture starts to dry out, you may need to add a little more stock.) Add the lemon juice and season to taste, then serve immediately.

Spring vegetable roast chicken

I don't think I'm alone in saying roast chicken is probably my favourite meal. It's rarely a good idea to mess around with something so well loved. For this recipe I simply roast all the vegetables in the same tin as the chicken so the flavours have a proper chance to get to know each other.

Serves 4–6

PREPARATION TIME
10 minutes

COOKING TIME
1½–2 hours

600g (1lb 5oz) new potatoes (unpeeled), larger ones halved

2 fennel bulbs, trimmed and each cut lengthways through the root into 6 wedges

350g (12oz) carrots, peeled and cut at an angle into 1–2cm (½–¾in) thick slices

10 cloves of garlic, peeled and left whole

50ml (2fl oz) olive oil

Salt and freshly ground black pepper

1 whole chicken

Small handful of sage leaves

1 lemon, halved

* Preheat the oven to 200°C (400°F), Gas mark 6.

* Place the potatoes in a roasting tin with the fennel, carrots, garlic and olive oil. Season with salt and pepper and toss together to mix.

* Remove and discard any excess fat from the cavity of the chicken, then place on top of the vegetables in the tin, season inside the cavity with salt and pepper and add the sage leaves. Squeeze half a lemon into the chicken cavity, then place the squeezed lemon half inside the cavity. Squeeze the remaining half lemon over the chicken and vegetables, then cut the squeezed lemon half into chunks and add to the vegetables.

* Place in the oven and cook for 1½–2 hours or until the legs feel loose when you gently tug them and the juices run clear when you insert a skewer into the chicken just below the thigh.

* Tip the juice into a gravy jug and skim off any fat. Allow the chicken to rest for 10 minutes, covered in foil and in a warm place, then carve and place on plates with the roasted vegetables.

Chicken open-pot roast

The idea of a pot roast is to cook all the ingredients together with the lid on to keep everything moist. In this version the vegetables and chicken are kept moist but, with the lid off, the skin of the chicken is allowed to become crisp and golden.

Serves 4

PREPARATION TIME
5 minutes

COOKING TIME
35–40 minutes

3 tbsp olive oil

1 chicken, jointed into pieces, or 4 chicken thighs or breasts (with the skin left on)

Salt and freshly ground black pepper

450g (1lb) new potatoes (unpeeled), larger ones halved

2 small leeks or 1 large leek, trimmed and cut into 3cm (1¼in) lengths

250ml (9fl oz) chicken stock

1 sprig of tarragon, plus 1 tbsp chopped tarragon

4 tbsp lemon juice

1 tbsp Dijon mustard

Large, wide casserole dish or ovenproof saucepan

* Preheat the oven to 220°C (425°F), Gas mark 7.
* Pour the olive oil into the casserole dish or saucepan on a high heat, then season the chicken pieces with salt and pepper and place, skin side down, in the hot oil. Cook for 4–5 minutes or until a deep golden brown, then turn over, so that the skin side is now on top, and add the potatoes and leeks. Season with salt and pepper and gently stir on the heat for a further 2 minutes, being careful to keep the chicken skin side up.
* Pour in the stock and add the sprig of tarragon. Bring to the boil, then place in the oven, uncovered, and cook for about 30 minutes or until the potatoes are tender and the chicken is cooked through. Remove from the oven, stir in the chopped tarragon, along with the lemon juice and mustard, and serve immediately.

Chicken and chorizo with rice

Rice soaks up the flavour of whatever liquid it's cooked in. With a plethora of ingredients, from chicken and chorizo to garlic and wine, this rice is positively saturated in the flavours it absorbs.

Serves 4–6

PREPARATION TIME
10 minutes

COOKING TIME
40 minutes

1 tbsp olive oil

300g (11oz) chorizo, cut into 1cm (½in) cubes

1kg (2lb 3oz) chicken thighs or drumsticks (with the skin left on)

Salt and freshly ground black pepper

2 small onions, peeled and finely chopped

8 cloves of garlic, peeled and finely sliced

300g (11oz) basmati rice

200ml (7fl oz) white wine

1 litre (1¾ pints) chicken or vegetable stock

2 tbsp chopped flat-leaf parsley

Large casserole dish or saucepan with a lid

* Pour the olive oil into the casserole dish or saucepan on a medium heat and, when hot, add the chorizo. Stir-fry for 3–4 minutes or until the chorizo releases its deep amber oils, then remove, leaving the oil in the pan, and set aside.

* Season the chicken pieces with salt and pepper, then add to the dish or pan and cook for 6–8 minutes or until well browned all over. Next, stir in the onions and garlic and fry for about 5 minutes or until the onions are softened and slightly browned.

* Add the rice and pour in the wine, then bring to a simmer and cook, uncovered, for 3–4 minutes or until slightly reduced. Pour in the stock and bring to the boil, then reduce the heat, season with salt and pepper, cover with a lid and cook for 15–20 minutes or until the rice is tender and has absorbed all the liquid. Stir in the parsley and serve immediately.

Chicken and couscous tagine

I love how this quite simple-seeming recipe uses just a few ingredients to make something absolutely fabulous. The spiciness of the saffron and cinnamon combines with the sweetness of the honey to transform this tagine into a dish that's so much more impressive than the sum of its parts.

Serves 4–6

PREPARATION TIME
15 minutes

COOKING TIME
35–45 minutes

110g (4oz) shelled whole almonds, chopped

100ml (3½fl oz) olive oil

4 skinless, boneless chicken breasts, cut into 2cm (¾in) chunks

Salt and freshly ground black pepper

2 onions, peeled and finely chopped

4 cloves of garlic, peeled and finely sliced

1 x 5cm (2in) cinnamon stick

Good pinch of saffron

1.3 litres (2 pints 3½fl oz) chicken stock

2 tbsp runny honey

400g (14oz) couscous

Large casserole dish or saucepan with a lid

* Place the almonds in the casserole dish or saucepan on a high heat and cook, tossing frequently, for 2–3 minutes or until they are lightly browned (taking care not to let them burn), then transfer to a bowl and set aside.

* Pour 2 tablespoons of olive oil into the dish or pan, still on a high heat, then season the chicken with salt and pepper and place in the hot oil. Fry, stirring frequently, for 3 minutes or until browned all over.

* Reduce the heat to medium–low and add the remaining olive oil, followed by the onions, garlic and cinnamon stick. Cover with a lid and cook, stirring, for 6–8 minutes or until the onions are soft and lightly browned.

* Add the saffron to the dish or pan, along with the stock, and stir in the honey. Bring to the boil, then reduce the heat, cover with a lid and simmer for 20–25 minutes, stirring occasionally.

* Stir in the couscous, cover again and cook for a further 3 minutes or just until the couscous is soft, then stir in the toasted almonds, taste for seasoning and serve in warmed bowls.

Chicken biryani

I love big, one-pot curries like this biryani, in which the rice absorbs all the flavour from the meat and spices. It puts plain boiled rice well and truly in the shade. The raisins add a touch of sweetness and the toasted almonds a nice contrast in texture.

Serves 4–6

PREPARATION TIME
15 minutes

COOKING TIME
30 minutes

5 green cardamom pods

300g (11oz) basmati rice

Salt and freshly ground black pepper

25g (1oz) butter

1 large onion, peeled and finely sliced

4 cloves of garlic, peeled and finely chopped

1 tbsp peeled and finely chopped root ginger

½ tsp turmeric

1 tsp ground cumin

1 tsp ground coriander

½ tsp cayenne pepper

1 bay leaf

1 x 5cm (2in) cinnamon stick

4 skinless, boneless chicken breasts or thighs, cut into bite-sized pieces

75g (3oz) raisins

800ml (1 pint 9fl oz) chicken stock

2 tbsp chopped coriander

4 tbsp flaked almonds

* To extract the cardamom seeds from the pods, place the pods on a chopping board, lay the flat side of a large knife flat side over the top and press down to lightly crush. Remove the seeds and discard the pods. Lightly crush the seeds in a pestle and mortar.

* Put the rice in a heatproof bowl, season with salt and cover with boiling water.

* Melt the butter in a large saucepan on a medium heat and, when foaming, add the onion, garlic, ginger, turmeric, cumin, coriander, cayenne pepper, bay leaf, cinnamon stick and crushed cardamom seeds. Cook, stirring occasionally, for 10 minutes or until the onion is softened and slightly browned. Add the chicken pieces and stir-fry for 3 minutes or until the chicken is opaque and cooked through.

* Drain the rice and rinse under cold running water, then stir into the saucepan along with the raisins. Pour in the stock, season with salt and pepper and stir all the ingredients together. Bring to the boil, then reduce the heat, cover with a lid and simmer for 8–10 minutes or until the rice is cooked.

* Remove from the heat, taste for seasoning, then stir in the coriander and flaked almonds. Divide between warmed bowls to serve.

Pot-roast duck legs with onions and root vegetables

Duck and potatoes are great friends. Duck fat is perhaps the potato's favourite cooking medium. Here the two form the basis of a perfect winter meal, while the sweetness of the caramelised onions offset the duck's natural richness.

Serves 4

PREPARATION TIME
10 minutes

COOKING TIME
1–1¼ hours

½ tbsp olive oil

4 duck legs, excess fat removed but with the skin left on

4 onions, peeled and halved through the root, each half cut lengthways into 4 wedges

4 sprigs of rosemary

Salt and freshly ground black pepper

6 floury potatoes, peeled and cut into 2cm (¾in) dice

6 small white turnips, peeled and cut into 1–2cm (½–¾in) dice

Large casserole dish or ovenproof saucepan with a lid

* Preheat the oven to 200°C (400°F), Gas mark 6.

* Pour the olive oil into the casserole dish or saucepan on a medium heat and, when hot, add the duck legs, skin side down, followed by the onions, rosemary and some salt and pepper.

* Cook for 4–5 minutes or until the skin is a rich golden brown, then tip in the potatoes and turnips, cover with a lid and cook in the oven for 1–1¼ hours, by which time the onions should be golden and the root vegetables and duck cooked through and tender.

Lamb and chickpea tagine

A tagine is the Moroccan name for both the dish and the pot it's cooked in. The pot has a steep cone-shaped lid, but, luckily, you don't need a tagine pot to make this recipe – a casserole dish or even just a saucepan with a lid will do just as well.

Serves 8–10

PREPARATION TIME
15 minutes

COOKING TIME
2¼ hours

3 tbsp sunflower oil

1kg (2lb 3oz) boneless shoulder of lamb, cut into 2–3cm (¾–1¾in) cubes, trimmed of fat or gristle

Salt and freshly ground black pepper

3 onions, peeled and finely sliced

6 cloves of garlic, peeled and finely sliced

3 tsp ground cumin

3 tsp ground coriander

1½ tsp cayenne pepper

1½ tsp smoked paprika

3 tbsp tomato paste

300g (11oz) dried apricots, chopped

1.5 litres (2½ pints) chicken stock

3 x 400g tins of chickpeas, drained and rinsed

3 tbsp runny honey

Large casserole dish or ovenproof saucepan with a lid

* Preheat the oven to 160°C (325°F), Gas mark 3.

* Pour the sunflower oil into the casserole dish or saucepan on a high heat, then season the lamb with salt and pepper and place the meat in the hot oil. Cook, stirring occasionally, for 3–4 minutes or until well browned all over.

* Reduce the heat to medium, then add the onions and garlic and fry, stirring occasionally, for 6–8 minutes or until the onions are softened and slightly browned. Stir in the cumin and coriander, cayenne pepper and paprika and cook for a further minute, then add the tomato paste, apricots and stock. Bring to the boil, then season with salt and pepper, cover with a lid and place in the oven.

* Cook for 1½ hours, then stir in the chickpeas and honey, return to the oven and cook for a further 30 minutes. Remove from the oven, taste for seasoning and serve with couscous (see page 333).

Leg of lamb with roasted vegetables

I love this way of cooking a leg of lamb. By roasting it on top of the parsnips and potatoes, these soak up all the juices and flavour of the meat. While the lamb rests, the heat is then increased to crisp up the vegetables. When you are buying the leg of lamb, ask your butcher to remove the aitchbone at the top of the leg and trim the knuckle from the end.

Serves 6–8

PREPARATION TIME
15 minutes

COOKING TIME
1¾–2 hours

1 x 3–4kg (6½–8¾lb) leg of lamb

Salt and freshly ground black pepper

750g (1lb 10oz) floury potatoes, peeled and cut into 7mm (⅜in) thick slices

3 parsnips (about 450g/1lb in total), peeled and cut into 7mm (⅜in) thick slices

3 red onions, peeled and cut into wedges 1cm (½in) thick

3 tsp thyme leaves or chopped rosemary leaves

3 tbsp olive oil

Redcurrant jelly or mint sauce, to serve

* Preheat the oven to 180°C (350°F), Gas mark 4.

* If necessary, remove the papery skin from the lamb, then, using a sharp knife, make long shallow scores in a criss-cross pattern in the fat, spacing the lines 2.5cm (1in) apart, and season well with salt and pepper.

* Place all the remaining ingredients in a large roasting tin and toss together, seasoning with salt and pepper. Spread everything out in the tin and place the lamb on a rack over the top (if you don't have a rack, place the lamb in the roasting tin and surround it with the vegetables). Place in the oven and roast for 1½ hours or until the lamb is cooked to your liking.

* Take the tin out of the oven and increase the heat to 220°C (425°F), Gas mark 7. Transfer the lamb to a large plate or a board sitting in a tray, cover with foil and leave to rest somewhere warm.

* Place the vegetables back in the oven and cook for another 20–30 minutes or until golden on top.

* About 10 minutes before the vegetables are ready, start carving the lamb. Then divide between plates, adding spoonfuls of the now golden vegetables, and serve with some redcurrant jelly or mint sauce.

Lamb shanks with potatoes and pearl barley

Every August for a few years running, I cooked for a wonderful American couple who owned a house in Ireland. On dull rainy days they would request this most comforting dish. It's very convenient to make as all the ingredients just go into the pot together and the only thing you have to think about after that is adding the potatoes.

Serves 4

PREPARATION TIME
10–15 minutes

COOKING TIME
3¾ hours

2 tbsp olive oil

4 lamb shanks

Salt and freshly ground black pepper

4 red onions, each peeled and cut into 6 wedges

4 cloves of garlic, peeled and finely chopped

4 tomatoes, cut into 2cm (¾in) chunks

1 tsp caster sugar

4 tbsp pearl barley (about 100g/3½oz)

500ml (18fl oz) chicken stock

About 1.3kg (3lb) floury potatoes, peeled and quartered

Large casserole dish or ovenproof saucepan with a lid

* Preheat the oven to 150°C (300°F), Gas mark 2.

* Pour the olive oil into the casserole dish or saucepan on a medium–high heat and season the lamb shanks with salt and pepper. When the oil is hot, add the shanks and cook for about 4 minutes on each side or until they begin to brown. Add all the remaining ingredients apart from the potatoes.

* Bring to the boil, then cover with a lid and place in the oven for 2½ hours. Add the potatoes, cover again and return to the oven for a further 50–60 minutes or until the potatoes are cooked and the lamb shanks meltingly tender.

Lamb and sweet potato curry

Sweet potato is a good vegetable to use in a curry as its inherent sweetness stands up well to the hot spiciness of the sauce.

Serves 4–6

PREPARATION TIME
20 minutes

COOKING TIME
1½–1¾ hours

8 green cardamom pods

1 tbsp sunflower oil

500g (1lb 2oz) boneless leg or shoulder of lamb, cut into 2–3cm (¾–1¼in) cubes, trimmed of fat

Salt and freshly ground black pepper

1 onion, peeled and sliced

4 cloves of garlic, peeled and finely chopped

1 tsp peeled and finely chopped root ginger

2 tsp ground coriander

2 tsp ground cumin

¼ tsp turmeric

½ tsp cayenne pepper

500ml (18fl oz) chicken stock

1 sweet potato (about 300g/11oz), peeled and cut into 2cm (¾in) cubes

75ml (3fl oz) natural yoghurt

Handful of chopped coriander, to serve

Large casserole dish or saucepan with a lid

* To extract the cardamom seeds from the pods, place the pods on a chopping board, lay the flat side of a large knife over the top and press down to lightly crush. Remove the seeds, discarding the pods, and set aside.

* Pour the sunflower oil into the casserole dish or saucepan on a high heat, then season the lamb with salt and pepper and place in the hot oil. Sauté the lamb pieces, stirring frequently, for 5 minutes or until the meat is browned all over. Remove the meat with a slotted spoon, leaving any oil behind, and set aside on a plate.

* Add a little extra sunflower oil to the dish or pan if necessary, then reduce the heat to medium and add the onion, garlic and ginger. Cook, stirring occasionally, for 6–8 minutes or until the onion is soft and golden. Next, stir in the coriander and cumin, along with the turmeric and cayenne pepper, and add the reserved lamb.

* Stir together for a further minute, then pour in the stock and season with salt and pepper. Bring to the boil, then reduce the heat to low, cover with a lid and simmer for 45 minutes to 1 hour, stirring occasionally, until the lamb is almost tender.

* Next, tip in the sweet potato and cook for another 30 minutes or until the potato is soft. If you would like a thicker sauce, then remove the lid and cook, uncovered, for a further 10 minutes. Remove from the heat, stir in the yoghurt and serve with a sprinkling of fresh coriander and naan bread.

Slow-roast shoulder of pork

It's true that this joint takes quite a while to cook, yet it really is fuss-free – the pork requires no attention as it slowly cooks in the oven. The long, slow roasting transforms this otherwise quite tough cut into a divine piece of meat. When pork is this tender, you don't need to carve it into slices, and nor would you be able to. Rather just pull off succulent shreds of the meat and pieces of crispy crackling and serve with the roasted vegetables.

Serves 6–8

PREPARATION TIME
10 minutes

COOKING TIME
6 hours 20 minutes

1 x 3–4kg (6½–8¾lb) pork shoulder on the bone

Salt and freshly ground black pepper

1 bulb of garlic, broken up into cloves (unpeeled)

1 butternut squash (about 900g/2lb) (unpeeled), deseeded and cut into 2–3cm (¾–1¼in) cubes

4 trimmed leeks (about 375g/13oz in total), cut into 2cm (¾in) thick slices

Small handful of sage leaves

* Preheat the oven to 220°C (425°F), Gas mark 7.

* Using a sharp knife, score the rind of the pork in a criss-cross pattern at 5mm (¼ in) intervals, cutting through the fat but not into the meat itself. (Or ask your butcher to do this for you, if you prefer.) Sprinkle over 1 tablespoon of salt, rubbing it into the lines scored in the fat, then place the pork in a large roasting tin and roast in the oven for 30 minutes. Reduce the temperature to 150°C (300°F), Gas mark 2 and continue to cook for a further 5 hours.

* After 5 hours, take the pork out of the oven and turn the temperature back up to 220°C (425°F), Gas mark 7. Pour off the fat into a bowl, leaving any juices in the tin. Place the garlic, squash, leeks and sage leaves around the pork. Then pour over 3 tablespoons of the reserved fat, season with salt and pepper and toss the vegetables together in the tin.

* Return to the oven for 40–50 minutes or until the pork rind has turned into delicious crackling and the vegetables are cooked through and golden. Serve as it is at the table or transfer to a large plate.

Spanish pork stew

The tomatoes, peppers and chorizo make this stew unmistakably Spanish. It's both simple to put together and bursting with flavour, while the vinegar provides an essential dose of acidity to contrast with the sweetness of the tomato, onion and red pepper.

Serves 6–8

PREPARATION TIME
10 minutes

COOKING TIME
2–2¼ hours

3 tbsp olive oil

1 x 950g (2lb 2oz) pork shoulder, cut into 2cm (¾in) cubes

Salt and freshly ground black pepper

200g (7oz) chorizo, cut into 1cm (½in) cubes

2 red peppers, deseeded and cut into 1cm (½in) cubes

2 onions, peeled and sliced

5 cloves of garlic, peeled and finely sliced

2 tbsp tomato purée

2 tbsp cider or red wine vinegar

400ml (14fl oz) chicken or vegetable stock

2 x 400g tins of chopped tomatoes

1 tsp granulated or caster sugar

800g (1¾lb) new potatoes (unpeeled), larger ones halved

* Preheat the oven to 160°C (325°F), Gas mark 3.

* Pour the olive oil into a large casserole dish or ovenproof saucepan with a lid on a high heat, season the pork with salt and pepper and, when hot, add the meat to the dish or pan. Fry, stirring frequently, for 5 minutes or until browned, then stir in the chorizo, red peppers, onions and garlic. Reduce the heat to medium and cook, stirring occasionally, for 6–8 minutes or until the onions are soft and lightly browned.

* Stir in the tomato purée with the vinegar, stock, tomatoes and sugar. Season with salt and pepper, then cover with a lid, bring to the boil and place in the oven. Cook for 1 hour, then remove from the oven, stir in the new potatoes and season with salt and pepper. Cook for a further 40–50 minutes or until the meat and potatoes are both tender. Taste for seasoning and serve.

Sausage and lentil stew

Lentils love pork more than any other meat. Here the vegetables, bacon and wine add body and depth to the dish and, combined with the sausages, make for a hearty winter supper.

Serves 4

PREPARATION TIME
10 minutes

COOKING TIME
1 hour

1 tbsp olive oil

150g (5oz) streaky bacon (in the piece or about 5 rashers), cut into 1–2cm (½–¾in) dice

4 cloves of garlic, peeled and crushed or finely grated

1 onion, peeled and sliced

1 stick of celery, trimmed and finely chopped

200g (7oz) Puy lentils

150ml (5fl oz) red wine

500ml (18fl oz) chicken stock

1 bay leaf

1 sprig of rosemary

8 pork sausages (about 300g/11oz in total)

Salt and freshly ground black pepper

To serve

2 tbsp chopped parsley

4 tbsp Parmesan cheese shavings

* Pour the olive oil into a large saucepan (ovenproof if cooking in the oven – see below) on a medium–high heat and, when hot, add the bacon. Fry for about 5 minutes or until most of the fat has rendered out and the bacon is lightly golden, then reduce the heat to medium–low, add the garlic, onion and celery and cook, stirring regularly, for another 10–15 minutes or until the onions are golden brown.

* Tip the lentils and the red wine into the pan, then bring to the boil and cook for 2–3 minutes or until the wine has almost evaporated.

* Add the stock, herbs and sausages, then bring back up to the boil, cover with a lid, reduce the heat to low and simmer for about 30 minutes or until the lentils are tender. Alternatively, place in the oven (preheated to 160°C/325°F/Gas mark 3) and bake for 30 minutes.

* Remove the herbs, season with salt and pepper to taste and serve with the chopped parsley and Parmesan shavings scattered over the top.

Provençal beef stew

A delicious and straightforward dish to throw together, this stew comes alive with the Provençal flavours of the herbs and olives. Like any stew, this recipe can be made a day or two in advance and reheated to serve.

Serves 4–6

PREPARATION TIME
10 minutes

COOKING TIME
2¼ hours

4 tbsp olive oil

2 onions, peeled and chopped

4 cloves of garlic, peeled and finely sliced

Salt and freshly ground black pepper

1kg (2lb 3oz) stewing beef, cut into 2cm (¾in) cubes

2 x 400g tins of chopped tomatoes

1 tsp caster sugar

700g (1½lb) new potatoes (unpeeled), larger ones halved

2 tbsp capers, drained and rinsed

2 tbsp pitted and chopped black olives

1 tbsp chopped thyme or rosemary leaves

Large casserole dish or ovenproof saucepan with a lid

* Preheat the oven to 160°C (325°F), Gas mark 3.

* Pour the olive oil into the casserole dish or saucepan on a medium–high heat and, when hot, add the onions and garlic and season with salt and pepper. Fry for 6–8 minutes or until the onions are soft and lightly golden.

* Tip in the beef and stir in the dish or pan for 2–3 minutes to brown the meat, then add the tomatoes and sugar. Bring to the boil, then cover with a lid and cook in the oven for 1 hour.

* Remove from the oven, season with a little more salt, then stir in the potatoes, cover and return to the oven for another hour or until the beef is tender and the potatoes are cooked through. Stir in the capers, olives and herbs, taste for seasoning and serve.

Beef pie

The pastry in this pie is a simple 'lid' added to the dish, rendering it easy to make and even easier to eat (see photographs on the next page).

Serves 8

PREPARATION TIME
20 minutes

COOKING TIME
2–2¾ hours

2 tbsp olive oil

900g (2lb) stewing beef, cut into 2cm (¾in) cubes

Salt and freshly ground black pepper

2 tbsp plain flour

2 onions, peeled and finely chopped

2 carrots, peeled and finely chopped

2 sticks of celery, trimmed and finely chopped

2 large leeks, trimmed and cut into 3cm (1¼in) lengths

4 cloves of garlic, peeled and finely sliced

2 tbsp tomato paste

200ml (2fl oz) red wine

2 tbsp red wine vinegar

2 strips of orange peel

1 bay leaf

2 sprigs of rosemary

200g (7oz) ready-rolled puff pastry (or see page 195)

1 egg, beaten

* Preheat the oven to 160°C (325°F), Gas mark 3.

* Pour the olive oil into a 28cm (11in) casserole dish on a medium–high heat, season the beef with salt and pepper and, when hot, add the meat to the pan. Fry, stirring frequently, for 3–4 minutes or until well browned, then stir in the flour and cook for a further minute.

* Add the chopped vegetables, garlic and tomato paste. Stir together and cook for another 5 minutes or until the vegetables have softened. Add the wine, vinegar, orange peel, bay leaf and rosemary, along with 300ml (½ pint) water. Season with salt and pepper, then stir together, bring to the boil and cover with a lid.

* Place in the oven and cook for 1¾–2¼ hours or until the beef is tender, then remove from the oven and increase the heat to 230°C (450°F), Gas mark 8.

* While the oven is heating up, cut the pastry to fit the top of the casserole dish, so that it is about 1cm (½in) wider all round. Roll out the trimmings and cut out shapes to decorate the top of the pastry, then scallop the edges of the 'lid' using the blunt side of a table knife to press it in at roughly 4cm (1½in) intervals all around the edge (see photographs on next page).

* Stick the cut-out shapes to the lid with beaten egg and brush them with a little more. Then make a hole about 3mm (⅛in) wide in the centre using the tip of a sharp knife (to allow the steam to escape during cooking and ensure the pastry stays crisp).

* Place the pastry on top of the filling (see next page), then return the dish to the oven and bake for a further 12–15 minutes or until the pastry is crisp and golden. Remove from the oven and serve.

Beef and red wine hot pot

Lancashire hot pot is a dish traditionally made using lamb. This variation replaces the lamb with beef while retaining the crust of sliced potatoes that absorbs the flavours of the rich stew beneath and turns crispy and golden on top. You can prepare in advance and keep covered, in the fridge, for up to 24 hours before cooking.

Serves 6

PREPARATION TIME
15 minutes

COOKING TIME
2–2½ hours

3 tbsp olive oil

250g (9oz) button mushrooms, halved (or quartered if they are larger)

Salt and freshly ground black pepper

2 small onions, peeled and sliced

4 cloves of garlic, peeled and finely chopped

1.5kg (3lb 5oz) stewing beef, cut into 6cm (2½in) chunks

150ml (5fl oz) red wine

3 tsp chopped thyme leaves

1 tbsp red wine vinegar

650g (1lb 7oz) floury potatoes, peeled and cut into 5mm (¼in) thick slices

25g (1oz) butter, diced

Large casserole dish or ovenproof saucepan with a lid

* Preheat the oven to 150°C (300°F), Gas mark 2.

* Pour the olive oil into the casserole dish or saucepan on a medium–high heat and, when hot, add the mushrooms. Season with salt and pepper and toss for 2–3 minutes or until lightly golden. Remove the mushrooms from the dish or pan and set aside, leaving any oil behind in the pan.

* If there isn't much oil left in the dish or pan, add another tablespoon. Tip in the onions and garlic, stir over the heat, then season with salt and pepper and cook for 4–5 minutes or until they start to turn golden at the edges.

* Add the meat and wine and 2 teaspoons of the thyme leaves. Bring to the boil, then cover with a lid and place in the oven to cook for 1¼–1½ hours or until the meat is just tender.

* Take the dish or pan out of the oven and turn up the heat to 230°C (450°F), Gas mark 8. Stir in the fried mushrooms and red wine vinegar, and add the potato slices, arranging them over the beef in the pan (it's fine if there's more than one layer). Scatter over the remaining thyme and some salt and pepper, then dot with the butter. Place back in the (now hot) oven and bake for a further 30–40 minutes or until the potatoes are cooked through and beginning to turn golden. Bring to the table and serve.

Caramel rice pudding

This is a slightly elaborate take on classic rice pudding, but that extra effort is absolutely worth it. First you make a caramel by heating the butter and sugar, then the milk is added and it dissolves the caramel, taking on a glorious flavour and gorgeous amber colour.

Serves 2–4 (v)

PREPARATION TIME
5 minutes

COOKING TIME
30–35 minutes

50g (2oz) butter

100g (3½oz) caster sugar

1.2 litres (2 pints) milk

¼–½ tsp salt

1 vanilla pod, split lengthways

100g (3½oz) short-grain pudding rice

Handful of shelled toasted hazelnuts, to decorate (optional) (see tip on page 281 for how to toast them yourself)

* Melt the butter in a large saucepan over a medium heat and when the butter starts to foam stir in 50g (2oz) of the sugar. Keep stirring over the heat for 3–4 minutes or until the mixture is smooth and has turned a dark caramel colour.

* Add the milk, whisking it into the mixture. The caramel will harden, but just keep whisking and it will dissolve into the milk.

* Add the remaining sugar, along with the salt, vanilla pod and rice. Bring to a simmer and continue to cook, stirring frequently, for 25–30 minutes or until the mixture has thickened.

* Meanwhile, if you are using unroasted hazelnuts to decorate, place them in a small frying pan on a high heat and cook, tossing frequently, for about 1 minute or until lightly browned (taking care not to let them burn). Lightly crush them with a pestle and mortar or place in a plastic bag and use a rolling pin to break them up, then set aside.

* When the rice pudding has finished cooking, taste, adding more sugar or salt if necessary, then serve, with a scattering of the toasted hazelnuts if you like.

Cinnamon baked apples

'Eating' apples hold their shape when cooked, making them ideal for this recipe as they can be soft but still stand firm when served.

Serves 6 (v)

PREPARATION TIME
5 minutes

COOKING TIME
1 hour

6 eating apples (unpeeled)

75g (3oz) dried apricots, finely chopped

75g (3oz) shelled pecan nuts, finely chopped

1½ tbsp soft light or dark brown sugar, plus extra for sprinkling

1½ tbsp ground cinnamon

* Preheat the oven to 160°C (325°F), Gas mark 3.
* First prepare the apples. Slice the top 1cm (½ in) off each apple and retain, then core each fruit with an apple corer and place in one of the holes of a 6-hole muffin tin.
* Mix together the remaining ingredients and use this mixture to fill the apples, adding extra to cover the top of each fruit. Replace the cut-off tops of the apples, then bake in the oven for about 1 hour or until the apples are soft all the way through. Serve with whipped cream or ice cream and a sprinkling of brown sugar.

Spiced plums in red wine

This is a really lovely way of cooking plums, the sweetness balanced by the spices and red wine.

Serves 4 (v)

PREPARATION TIME
2 minutes

COOKING TIME
8–10 minutes

4 large plums, halved and stones removed

120ml (4½fl oz) red wine

Juice of 1 large orange

100g (3½oz) caster sugar

2 cloves

1 x 5cm (2in) cinnamon stick

* Place all the ingredients in a saucepan and stir. Cover with a lid and bring to a simmer, cooking on a medium heat for 8–10 minutes or until the plums are softened.
* Discard the cloves and cinnamon, then divide between plates and serve with a dollop of Greek yoghurt or vanilla ice cream.

Pear, almond and chocolate crumble

More than just a crumble, this dessert unites pears with two of its favourite companions – almonds and chocolate.

Serves 8–10 (v)

PREPARATION TIME
15 minutes

COOKING TIME
50–55 minutes

12 pears (about 900g/2lb in total), peeled, cored and cut into 2cm (¾in) cubes

2 tbsp caster sugar

75g (3oz) plain flour

1 tbsp ground cinnamon (optional)

75g (3oz) ground almonds

75g (3oz) butter, chilled and diced

75g (3oz) dark chocolate, roughly chopped, or dark chocolate drops

75g (3oz) soft light brown sugar

2 litre (3½ pint) pie dish

* Preheat the oven to 180°C (350°F), Gas mark 4.

* Add the pears and the caster sugar to the pie dish, stir to mix and then place in the oven. Bake for about 10 minutes or until the pears have softened, then remove from the oven and set aside.

* Next, make the crumble. Sift the flour and cinnamon (if using) into a large bowl, add the ground almonds and butter and, using your fingertips, rub it in until the mixture resembles very coarse breadcrumbs. (Don't rub it in too much or the crumble won't be crunchy.) Add the chocolate and sugar and mix to combine.

* Sprinkle the crumble mixture over the slightly cooled pears, pushing down any chocolate pieces that are sitting on top. Place the crumble in the oven and bake for 40–45 minutes or until browned on top. Serve warm with whipped cream or vanilla ice cream.

Chocolate croissant bread and butter pudding

I'm afraid this pudding is not even close to being fat-free. It's unapologetically indulgent. This is not to be made every day but I urge you to try it. Outrageously rich it may be, it's also outrageously good.

Serves 6–8 (v)

PREPARATION TIME
5 minutes

COOKING TIME
45 minutes

125g (4½oz) dark chocolate, broken into pieces, or dark chocolate drops

6 croissants (slightly stale is fine)

4 eggs

450ml (16fl oz) single or regular cream

250ml (9fl oz) milk

150g (5oz) caster sugar, plus extra for sprinkling

1 tsp vanilla extract

Pinch of salt

2 litre (3½ pint) pie dish

* Preheat the oven to 180°C (350°F), Gas mark 4.

* Scatter half the chocolate over the base of the pie dish. Cut the croissants in half and lay them, cut side down and slightly overlapping, in the dish, then scatter over the remaining chocolate.

* In a bowl, whisk together the remaining ingredients and pour this mixture over the croissants. Sprinkle with 1 tablespoon of sugar and allow to stand for 5 minutes before baking in the oven for about 45 minutes or until the custard is just set in the centre. Remove from the oven and serve (if you dare!) with softly whipped cream.

No Cook

Cooking doesn't always have to mean 'heat' and there are a few good reasons to do without it. Raw food is perfect if you want something fresh and light. No cook recipes will also save you time, as you don't need to wait for anything to warm up. Even better, most of these recipes, like the gazpachos and salads, are extremely healthy. I've also included quite a few recipes to serve on bread or toast which are much more than a sandwich, they're a meal in themselves. You'll also find classic but elegant raw-food dishes such as ceviche and salmon tartare, which are perfect for serving to guests on a summer's evening. So whatever your reason for not getting out the pots and pans, you'll find plenty of inspiration here.

Beetroot gazpacho

The flavour of this cold soup is as intense as its beautiful colour. It is perfect to serve as a starter in the summer when the sun is shining, tomatoes are at their best and beetroot is young, small and tender. This recipe is similar to a dish served at the fabulous Moro restaurant in London, which serves food inspired by the cuisine of Spain, North Africa and the Mediterranean.

Serves 4–6 (v)

PREPARATION TIME
10 minutes

500g (1lb 2oz) cherry tomatoes, halved

110g (4oz) cucumber, left unpeeled and roughly chopped

1 red pepper, deseeded and roughly chopped

2 spring onions, trimmed and roughly chopped

300g (11oz) raw beetroot, peeled and roughly chopped

2 small cloves of garlic, peeled and crushed or finely grated

4 tbsp olive oil

2–4 tsp sherry vinegar

Salt and freshly ground black pepper

* Place all the vegetables and the garlic in a food processor and whiz for at least 3 minutes or until the mixture is completely smooth. Pour the puréed ingredients into a fine sieve set over a bowl and press down against the mixture with the back of a spoon to help push the liquid through. Discard the pulp left in the sieve.

* Stir in the olive oil and season to taste with the sherry vinegar, salt and pepper. Serve at room temperature or chilled from the fridge with a grinding of black pepper and some crusty bread.

White gazpacho

This gazpacho is a lovely cold soup. It is deceptively simple and the flavour is stunning – a combination of almonds and garlic with a hint of acidity from the vinegar. The soup is a gorgeous creamy colour, which looks beautiful decorated with a few drops of golden olive oil.

Serves 4 (v)

PREPARATION TIME
10 minutes

100g (3½oz) blanched almonds

1 clove of garlic, peeled and crushed or finely grated

250ml (9fl oz) ice-cold water

25g (1oz) (about 1 slice) white bread, crusts removed

2 tbsp olive oil, plus extra for drizzling

1 tbsp sherry vinegar

Salt and freshly ground black pepper

Crushed ice, to serve (optional)

* Whiz the almonds in a food processor for 2 minutes, then add the garlic and 2 tablespoons of the iced water and whiz for a further 2 minutes. Add the bread, olive oil and remaining water, then blitz for another 3 minutes or until smooth.

* Stir in the sherry vinegar and season to taste with salt and pepper. Divide between small bowls or glasses, drizzling ½ teaspoon of olive oil into each one and adding a grinding of black pepper. Serve with crushed ice, if you like.

Fennel and pink grapefruit with feta

Fennel is delicious either cooked or raw. When cooked it is juicy and soft, but when raw – as in this salad – it provides a snappy freshness to go with its lovely aniseed flavour.

Serves 4–6 (v)

PREPARATION TIME
10 minutes

2 pink grapefruit

2 fennel bulbs, trimmed and cut into 1cm (½in) dice

2 tsp caster sugar

200g (7oz) feta cheese, cut into 1cm (½in) cubes

2 tbsp chopped mint

Olive oil, for drizzling

Freshly ground black pepper

* To peel the grapefruit, first cut a slice off the top and the bottom of each one, cutting through just below the pith and into the flesh. Place the grapefruit on a plate (to collect the juice) and, using a small sharp knife, slice off the peel in strips following the curvature of the fruit. Cut away any white pith, leaving as much of the flesh as possible.

* Once the grapefruit are peeled, slice them crossways into rounds about 1cm (½in) thick, then slice each of these into quarters.

* Tip the chopped grapefruit and any juice into a wide serving bowl, add the fennel and the sugar and toss together. Scatter over the feta and mint and serve drizzled with a little olive oil and a grinding of black pepper.

Fennel and mango salad

Well-balanced ingredients are what make this simple salad so effective. The crisp fennel and crunchy hazelnuts complement the soft mango, whose sweetness contrasts with the salty feta. Serve for a light lunch or starter.

Serves 4–6 (v)

PREPARATION TIME
10 minutes

Large handful of shelled toasted hazelnuts

2 mangoes, peeled, stone removed and flesh cut into 1cm (½in) cubes or 5mm (¼in) slices

2 fennel bulbs, trimmed and cut lengthways into thin slices

100ml (3½fl oz) olive oil

2 tbsp lemon juice

4 tbsp chopped mint

Salt and freshly ground black pepper

250g (9oz) feta cheese

* Lightly crush the hazelnuts with a pestle and mortar or place in a plastic bag and use a rolling pin to break them up, then set aside.

* In a bowl, mix together the mango and fennel with the olive oil, lemon juice and mint. To serve, season with salt and pepper, then divide between plates, scatter over the toasted hazelnuts and crumble over the feta cheese.

Rachel's tip

If you can't get ready toasted hazelnuts, then you can toast them fresh. To do this, place the hazelnuts in a small frying pan on a high heat and cook, tossing frequently, for about 1 minute or until lightly browned (taking care not to let them burn).

Parma ham and nectarine salad

Dry-cured ham is a real favourite of mine. Due to the curing and air-drying process its flavour is wonderfully concentrated and acts as a terrific foil to green salads.

2 nectarines or peaches (unpeeled), stone removed and flesh cut into 5mm (¼in) thick slices

4 slices of Parma ham, torn into pieces

4 handfuls of mixed salad leaves, such as rocket or lettuce

4 tbsp olive oil

2 tbsp lemon juice

4 tbsp chopped mint

Serves 4

PREPARATION TIME
5 minutes

* Arrange all the ingredients on a plate or toss together in a bowl, carefully dividing between plates to serve.

Pear and blue cheese salad

Blue cheese has a distinctive intense salty flavour that can really perk up a dish. Here it contrasts well with the sweetness of the pear, while the pecans provide a most welcome crunch.

4 tbsp olive oil

2 tbsp cider vinegar

2 tsp runny honey

2 tsp Dijon mustard

Salt and freshly ground black pepper

4 handfuls of mixed salad leaves

2 pears, peeled, cored and cut into 3mm (⅛in) thick slices

110g (4oz) blue cheese, cut into 1cm (½in) cubes

50g (2oz) shelled pecan nuts, roughly chopped

Serves 4 (v)

PREPARATION TIME
5 minutes

* In a bowl, mix together the olive oil, vinegar, honey and mustard. Season with salt and pepper, then toss in the salad leaves, pear slices and blue cheese.

* Divide the salad between plates, then sprinkle with the chopped pecans to serve.

Mashed chickpeas on toast

My cupboard is rarely without a tin of chickpeas. They are almost as good from a tin as they are cooked fresh. Chickpeas taste great mashed on toast and drizzled with paprika oil; the strong, smoky flavour makes them come alive.

Serves 4 (v)

PREPARATION TIME
5 minutes

2 x 400g tins of chickpeas, drained and rinsed

Finely grated zest of 2 lemons

2 tbsp chopped mint

2 small cloves of garlic, peeled and crushed or finely grated

120ml (4½fl oz) olive oil

½ tsp smoked paprika

To serve

4 slices of bread

30g (1¼oz) butter

* In a bowl, mix together the chickpeas with the lemon zest, mint, garlic and 3 tablespoons of olive oil. Use a fork or potato masher to mash together the chickpeas until well broken up but not completely smooth.

* Toast the bread on both sides, then butter it and spread with the mashed chickpeas. Mix together the paprika with the remaining olive oil, drizzle a teaspoon or two of the gorgeous red oil onto the chickpeas and serve.

Artichoke purée on toast

This is a purée my husband Isaac likes to make – it is quick to whiz up but packed full of flavour and delicious on toast.

150g (5oz) preserved artichoke hearts (from a jar or tin)

4 tbsp olive oil

Squeeze of lemon juice

30g (1¼oz) Parmesan cheese, finely grated

Salt and freshly ground black pepper

To serve

4 slices of bread

30g (1¼oz) butter

Shavings of Parmesan cheese

Serves 4

PREPARATION TIME
5 minutes

* Place the artichokes in a food processor with the olive oil, lemon juice and Parmesan and whiz for 1–2 minutes or until smooth. Season.

* Toast the bread on both sides (or leave untoasted), then butter, spoon over the purée and scatter over a few Parmesan shavings to serve.

Chicken with basil mayonnaise on toast

Mayonnaise happily accommodates many different flavours and ingredients, and is perfect with cooked chicken.

200g (7oz) cooked chicken, cut into bite-sized pieces

200ml (7fl oz) mayonnaise

6 tbsp chopped basil

2 tomatoes (about 200g/7oz), chopped

Salt and freshly ground black pepper

To serve

4 slices of bread

30g (1¼oz) butter

Serves 4

PREPARATION TIME
5 minutes

* In a bowl, mix all the ingredients together, seasoning to taste with salt and pepper.

* Toast the bread on both sides (or leave untoasted), then butter it and spread over the chicken mixture to serve.

Mixed root remoulade with ham

Here is an earthy take on the classic deli combination of ham and coleslaw.

100g (3½oz) celeriac, peeled and coarsely grated

100g (3½oz) parsnips, peeled and coarsely grated

100g (3½oz) carrots, peeled and coarsely grated

3 tbsp mayonnaise

1 tsp Dijon mustard

Juice of ½ lemon

Salt and freshly ground black pepper

To serve

6 slices of bread

25g (1oz) butter

10–12 slices of cooked ham

Serves 6

PREPARATION TIME

15 minutes

* In a bowl, mix together all the salad ingredients, seasoning to taste with salt and pepper.

* Toast the bread on both sides (or leave untoasted) and butter it, then place on plates, spoon over the salad and serve with the ham.

Thai crab toast

Most fishmongers and many supermarkets sell good-quality freshly cooked crab meat, which I would recommend for this dish.

350g (12oz) pre-cooked crab meat

1 tsp fish sauce (nam pla)

½ tsp peeled and finely grated root ginger

2 tbsp chopped coriander

1 avocado, peeled and cut into 1cm (½in) cubes

Juice of 1–2 limes

To serve

4 slices of bread

Sesame oil, for drizzling

Serves 4

PREPARATION TIME
5 minutes

* Place the crab meat in a bowl, along with the fish sauce, ginger, coriander, avocado and the juice of 1 lime. Mix all the ingredients together, adding more lime juice if necessary.
* Toast the bread on both sides and drizzle over a good few drops of sesame oil before spreading with the crab mixture and serving.

Spiced chicken open sandwich

I love this twist on a chicken sandwich: the garam masala gives a spiciness to the mayonnaise and the cashews a delicious crunch.

200g (7oz) cooked chicken, cut into bite-sized pieces

200ml (7fl oz) mayonnaise

4 tsp garam masala (to make your own, see page 129)

1 stick of celery, trimmed and finely sliced

50g (2oz) roasted cashew nuts

Salt and freshly ground black pepper

To serve

4 slices of bread

30g (1¼oz) butter

Serves 4

PREPARATION TIME
5 minutes

* Place all the ingredients in a bowl and season with salt and pepper.
* Toast the bread on both sides (or leave untoasted), then butter it and spread with the spicy chicken mixture to serve.

Ceviche

Ceviche is raw fish marinated in lime juice, the acid in the juice effectively 'cooking' the fish. Use the freshest fish available.

500g (1lb 2oz) skinless white fish fillets, such as pollock, haddock, cod, plaice or sole, cut into strips 5mm (¼in) thick

Juice of 6 limes

3 spring onions, trimmed and sliced

150g (5oz) cucumber, peeled and cut into 5mm (¼in) dice

2 avocados, peeled, stone removed and flesh cut into 5mm (¼in) dice

½–1 red chilli, deseeded and finely chopped

Lime slices, to serve

Serves 4–6

PREPARATION TIME
10 minutes, plus chilling

* Place the fish pieces in a large bowl, add the lime juice and mix together, then cover with cling film or a plate and leave in the fridge to chill for at least 1 hour.
* Remove from the fridge and mix in the remaining ingredients. Divide between plates, add lime slices and serve.

Smoked salmon and avocado on rye toast

Strong-flavoured and dark in colour, rye bread is becoming more readily available. Brown bread is a good alternative.

200g (7oz) smoked salmon, cut into bite-sized pieces

2 small avocados, peeled, stone removed and flesh diced

1 small red onion, peeled and finely chopped

2 tbsp chopped basil

2 tbsp chopped mint

2 tbsp crème fraîche

Salt and freshly ground black pepper

To serve

4 slices of rye bread

30g (1¼oz) butter

Serves 4

PREPARATION TIME
10 minutes

* In a bowl, mix all the ingredients together, seasoning to taste with salt and pepper.
* Toast the bread on both sides (or leave untoasted) and butter it, then top with the salmon and avocado mixture to serve.

Japanese-style salmon tartare

As the popularity of sushi grows, people here in the West are becoming much more familiar with eating raw fish. This fish tartare, with its Japanese flavourings, has echoes of sushi. As well as being supremely healthy, it's a brilliant a way of preserving the fish's fresh flavour all the way to the plate.

Serves 4

PREPARATION TIME
10 minutes

4 pea-sized blobs of wasabi (Japanese horseradish)

1½ tsp peeled and freshly grated root ginger

1 tbsp lime juice

125g (4½oz) cucumber, cut into 5mm (¼in) dice

350g (12oz) ultra-fresh salmon fillet, skin removed and flesh cut into 1cm (½in) dice

2 tsp toasted (or black) sesame seeds

2 tsp snipped chives

One 7–8cm (2¾–3in) cooking ring mould (see tip, right)

* In a bowl, mix together the wasabi, ginger and lime juice, followed by the cucumber and salmon, being careful not to break up the fish.

* Place the ring in the centre of a plate and fill with a quarter of the mixture to a depth of 2–3cm (¾–1¼ in), then repeat with the remaining portions. Scatter over the toasted sesame seeds and chives and serve.

Rachel's tip

If you don't have cooking rings, then it's easy to improvise and make them yourself. Simply cut up a used plastic ½-litre drinking bottle, snipping it into a ring, about 4cm (1½ in) deep.

Smoked mackerel, apple and fennel salad

Mackerel is seriously good for you and also seriously delicious. Smoked mackerel makes a lovely addition to a salad.

2 fennel bulbs, trimmed and cut lengthways into 3–4mm (⅛in) thick slices

2 apples (unpeeled), quartered, cored and cut into wedges 5mm (¼in) thick

4 smoked mackerel fillets, skin removed and flesh torn into bite-sized chunks

4 handfuls of salad leaves, such as rocket or lettuce

5 tbsp olive oil

2 tbsp lemon juice

Salt and freshly ground black pepper

Serves 4–6

PREPARATION TIME
10 minutes

* Place all the ingredients in a serving bowl and gently toss together.
* Season to taste with salt and pepper, and serve directly from the bowl or on individual plates.

Sardines on toast with basil and rocket

Sardines are packed with highly nutritious omega-3 oils. While fresh sardines taste fabulous, tinned sardines are an excellent substitute in many dishes.

2 x 100g tins of sardines, drained and cut into 2cm (¾in) pieces

2 tomatoes, cut into 1cm (½in) dice

4 tbsp finely sliced or torn basil leaves

2 tsp balsamic vinegar

4 tbsp olive oil

4 slices of sourdough bread

4 handfuls of rocket leaves

Salt and freshly ground black pepper

Serves 4

PREPARATION TIME
5 minutes

* In a bowl, gently mix the sardines, tomatoes and basil with the balsamic vinegar and half the olive oil.
* Meanwhile, toast the bread and drizzle over the remaining olive oil. Add the rocket leaves, top with the sardine mixture and season before serving.

Oranges with honey, pistachios and mint

Wonderfully refreshing, this dish sings of the Middle East. Eat it on its own after a rich meal, or with a blob of creamy thick yoghurt. If you're preparing this a few hours in advance, cover and keep it in the fridge and sprinkle over the pistachios just before serving.

Serves 4 (v)

PREPARATION TIME
10 minutes

4 oranges

1 tbsp runny honey

Pinch of ground cinnamon

1 tbsp chopped mint

25g (1oz) shelled pistachios, roughly chopped

* To peel the oranges, first cut a slice off the top and bottom of each orange, slicing through just below the pith and into the flesh. One by one, peel the oranges over a plate to collect the juice. Using a small sharp knife, slice off the peel in strips following the curvature of the fruit. Cut away any white pith, leaving as much of the flesh as possible.

* Once the oranges are peeled, slice them crossways into rounds about 5mm (¼ in) thick and lay them out flat in a wide shallow bowl.

* Tip any orange juice from the plate into a small bowl and mix with the honey, cinnamon and chopped mint. Pour this mixture over the oranges and scatter with the pistachios just before serving.

Quick banana ice cream

This is a superbly quick way of adding banana flavour to ice cream. I've used chocolate ice cream here, which works especially well, though you can use vanilla or even toffee. This would be great used in either of the sundaes on pages 57 and 58.

Serves 4 (v)

PREPARATION TIME
**3 minutes,
plus freezing**

300g (11oz) chocolate ice cream

1 small ripe banana, peeled and sliced

* First put a freezer-proof container or bowl in the freezer and leave for 5 minutes. Place the ice cream and banana in a food processor and whiz for 1 minute (or mash the banana with a fork and fold into the slightly softened ice cream), then quickly transfer to the ice-cold container or bowl and place back in the freezer.

* Leave to freeze for at least 30 minutes, then serve on its own or with toasted nuts and curls of dark chocolate or one of the toppings below.

Quick things to put on ice cream

Toasted nuts are a favourite of mine, plus a drizzling of something intense, such as maple syrup, honey or a sweet liqueur. Here are a few combinations I like to use. You can use ready-toasted nuts, for convenience, but they taste much better if you toast them yourself.

- A shot of espresso coffee with a scattering of toasted, lightly crushed/chopped hazelnuts.

- A sprinkling of toasted desiccated coconut and a little finely grated lime zest.

- A few glugs of maple syrup and some toasted pecan nuts.

- A spoonful of runny honey and a few chopped dates.

- Crystallised or stem ginger with a spoonful of the syrup.

- A splash of liqueur and a scattering of toasted nuts or grated chocolate, such as amaretto with toasted flaked almonds; a coffee liqueur (Tia Maria or Kahlúa) with toasted, lightly crushed hazelnuts; or an orange liqueur (triple sec or Cointreau) with curls of grated dark chocolate.

- A drizzling of a sweet sherry such as Pedro Ximénez or a handful of raisins soaked in sherry.

Little banoffee pots

These little desserts are quick to assemble and provide just the right mixture of sweetness, creaminess and crunch. They can be made an hour or two in advance, if you wish, and kept chilled in the fridge until you're ready to serve.

Makes 4 (v)

PREPARATION TIME
10 minutes

75ml (3fl oz) double or regular cream, plus an extra 2 tbsp

100ml (3½fl oz) dulce de leche (or boiled condensed milk – see recipe introduction, page 46)

6 digestive biscuits, broken into chunks

2 bananas, peeled and cut into 5mm (¼in) thick slices

four glasses

* Pour the cream into a bowl and whip into soft peaks. Place the dulce de leche in a separate bowl, mix in the extra 2 tablespoons of cream to thin it and then fold in the whipped cream.

* Divide half the biscuit pieces between the glasses, then add half the banana slices, dividing them between the glasses, followed by half the cream mixture.

* Repeat the layering with the remaining ingredients reserving a couple of slices of banana and some biscuit crumbs to top the pots.

Amaretto tiramisu

With its sweet almond flavour, amaretto is one of my favourite liqueurs. This quick, no-cook tiramisu uses amaretto to enhance the natural almond flavour of the amaretti biscuits. If you don't have amaretto, you can also use brandy. Please note that this recipe uses a raw egg, so isn't suitable for the elderly or pregnant.

Serves 4 (v)

PREPARATION TIME
**10 minutes,
plus chilling**

75ml (3fl oz) strong coffee, cooled

4 tbsp amaretto or brandy

40 amaretti biscuits (about 85g/3oz in total)

1 egg, separated

50g (2oz) caster sugar

125g (4½oz) mascarpone

1 tbsp cocoa powder

four glasses or bowls

* Pour the coffee and amaretto or brandy in a bowl. Add half the biscuits and allow to soak for a couple of minutes.

* Meanwhile, place the egg yolk, sugar and mascarpone in a separate bowl and whisk together for 3–4 minutes or until light and fluffy. In another, spotlessly clean bowl, whisk the egg white until it forms soft peaks and then carefully fold into the mascarpone mixture.

* Divide the soaked biscuits between the glasses or bowls. Next, divide approximately half the egg and mascarpone mixture between the glasses, then sift a little of the cocoa powder into each one.

* Repeat with the remaining ingredients to make a second layer of everything. Serve immediately or keep covered in the fridge (for several hours or overnight) until you are ready to serve.

St Clement's syllabub

Syllabub is a traditional creamy dessert that goes back to Tudor times. It is simple to make and a pleasure to eat. For better or worse, it is also quite uncompromisingly alcoholic.

Juice and finely grated zest of ½ orange

Juice and finely grated zest of ½ lemon

50g (2oz) caster sugar

50ml (2fl oz) Cointreau

300ml (½ pint) double or regular cream

four glasses

Serves 4 (v)

PREPARATION TIME
10 minutes, plus chilling

* Place all the ingredients apart from the cream in a bowl and mix together a little so the sugar starts to dissolve.

* In a separate bowl, whip the cream until it forms soft peaks. Fold in the sugary juice until well mixed, then divide between the glasses and chill in the fridge for 20–30 minutes or until set.

Melon with vodka, orange and mint

Wonderfully refreshing, this will be a welcome dessert after even the richest of meals.

1 small or ½ large melon, such as honeydew or charentais, peeled, deseeded and cut into 2cm (¾in) chunks

2 tbsp chopped mint

50ml (2fl oz) vodka

Juice of 1 orange

2 tsp caster sugar

four glasses or bowls

Serves 4 (v)

PREPARATION TIME
5 minutes

* Simply mix together all the ingredients, divide between the glasses or bowls and serve.

Strawberries with amaretti

A fresh summer strawberry is a magnificent fruit. Often just a drizzle of cream will suffice, though the almond notes in this dessert – from the amaretto liqueur and amaretti biscuits – really complement the fruit.

Serves 4 (v)

PREPARATION TIME
**10 minutes,
plus chilling**

150ml (5fl oz) double or
regular cream

3 tbsp amaretto

250g (9oz) strawberries,
hulled and finely sliced

25g (1oz) caster sugar

75g (3oz) amaretti
biscuits, broken into
rough chunks

four glasses

* Whip the cream until stiff peaks begin to appear, then fold in the amaretto. Toss the strawberries in the sugar.

* Spoon 1 tablespoon of the chilled amaretto cream into the bottom of each glass, followed by a tablespoon of the amaretti pieces and a tablespoon of the strawberries.

* Add another layer of cream, biscuits and strawberries, finishing with a dollop of cream and sprinkling of biscuits on the top of each glass. Serve straightaway or keep, covered, in the fridge for up to 6 hours.

Messes

Eton mess is a traditional English dessert made with fresh strawberries, meringue and whipped cream. It is an irresistible combination but here are a few variations to seduce you.

For the base

200ml double cream

50g (2oz) meringue (bought or homemade – see Rhubarb and Ginger Meringues, page 209), broken into bite-sized chunks

Fruit mixture of choice (see below)

four small bowls or large glasses

Serves 4 (v)

PREPARATION TIME
10 minutes

* Pour the cream into a bowl and whip into soft peaks.

* Fold in the meringue pieces and your chosen fruit mixture (see below), then divide between the bowls or glasses and serve.

Banoffee mess

1 large banana, peeled and cut into 1–2cm (½–¾in) dice

2 generous tbsp toffee sauce (see page 58) or dulce de leche (or boiled condensed milk – see recipe introduction, page 46)

* Simply mix together the banana and toffee sauce or dulce de leche before folding in with the meringue and cream, as above.

Blueberry mess

110g (4oz) fresh or frozen (and defrosted) blueberries

2 tsp caster sugar

* Mix most of the blueberries with the sugar and mash lightly with a fork, then fold in with the meringue and whipped cream, as above. Decorate with the remaining blueberries.

Mango and raspberry mess

50g (2oz) raspberries

2–4 tsp caster sugar

½ ripe mango, peeled and cut into cubes

* Mix together the raspberries with the sugar, taste for sweetness, adding more sugar if necessary. Then fold in with the meringue, whipped cream and mango pieces.

Fuss-free Extras and Sides

These easy extras and side dishes will go with many of the recipes throughout the book, or any of your other favourite dishes. They are simple and straightforward, and can round off any meal.

Roasted sweet potatoes

The sweet flavour and vibrant colour of sweet potato makes it an ideal accompaniment for meat such as pork or chicken.

Serves 4 (v)

PREPARATION TIME
10 minutes

COOKING TIME
30–40 minutes

50g (2oz) butter, melted

1 tbsp runny honey

2 tsp lemon juice

1kg (2lb 3oz) sweet potatoes, peeled and cut into 3cm (1¼in) chunks

Salt and freshly ground black pepper

* Preheat the oven to 180°C (350°F), Gas mark 4.

* In a bowl, mix together the butter with the honey and lemon juice, add the sweet potato chunks, season with salt and pepper and toss to coat. Tip into a roasting tin and spread out in a single layer, then roast in the oven for 30–40 minutes or until the sweet potatoes are soft and lightly browned.

Roasted new potatoes

Boiling potatoes before roasting softens them up in the middle, while the roasting gives them a gorgeous crunch. Here they are also tossed in semolina, a coarse flour, for added texture.

Serves 4–6 (v)

PREPARATION TIME
3 minutes

COOKING TIME
35–45 minutes

75ml (3fl oz) olive oil

Salt and freshly ground black pepper

1kg (2lb 3oz) new potatoes (unpeeled)

1 tbsp semolina

* Preheat the oven to 220°C (425°F), Gas mark 7. Pour the olive oil into a roasting tin and place in the oven to heat up.

* Fill a large saucepan with water, add a good pinch of salt and bring to the boil, then tip in the potatoes and cook for just 5 minutes before draining. Lightly crush the potatoes with a fork, keeping their shape but breaking the skin in places.

* Add the potatoes and the semolina to the hot roasting tin, toss to coat the potatoes in the oil and semolina and season well with salt and pepper. Place in the oven and roast for 30–40 minutes or until the potatoes are golden, turning them a couple of times during cooking to ensure they brown evenly.

Perfect mashed potatoes

For the best mashed potato, use a 'floury' variety, such as Kerr's Pink or Golden Wonder. To get the maximum goodness and flavour, it's best to peel them after boiling (floury potatoes tend to disintegrate if you peel them before boiling). If you make your mash in advance, add a little extra milk so it doesn't dry out as it sits. It keeps, covered, in a warm oven for an hour or so.

Serves 4 (v)

PREPARATION TIME
10 minutes

COOKING TIME
30–40 minutes

1kg (2lb 3oz) floury
potatoes (unpeeled),
scrubbed clean

Salt and freshly ground
black pepper

150ml (5fl oz) milk, or
110ml (4fl oz) milk and
50ml (2fl oz) single or
regular cream

25g (1oz) butter

* Fill a large saucepan with water, then add the potatoes and a good pinch of salt. Bring to the boil for 10 minutes, then pour all but about 4cm (1½ in) of the water out of the pan and continue to cook the potatoes on a very low heat. (Don't be tempted to stick a knife into them as the skins will break and they will disintegrate.)

* Continue to cook for another 20–30 minutes until a skewer goes in easily. Drain the potatoes, peel while they are still hot and put into a bowl to mash immediately by hand, or use the paddle attachment in an electric food mixer, until they are free of lumps.

* Bring the milk (or milk and cream) to the boil in a small saucepan. Add the butter and some salt and pepper to the potatoes. Add the boiling liquid and stir to a smooth consistency. You might not need all the milk/cream or you might need a little more – it depends on how dry the potatoes are. Taste for seasoning. Serve immediately or return the mash to a saucepan for reheating if not eating straightaway.

Variations

Horseradish mash: Stir 2 tablespoons of freshly grated horseradish into the finished mash.

Mustard and parsley mash: Stir 2 tablespoons each of Dijon mustard and chopped fresh parsley into the finished mash.

Olive oil and Parmesan mash: Replace the butter with 50ml (2fl oz) olive oil and 3 tablespoons of freshly grated Parmesan cheese.

Sautéed potatoes

This is one of the fastest ways of cooking potatoes; cutting them into small dice means they take only minutes to prepare.

Serves 4–6 (v)

PREPARATION TIME
5 minutes

COOKING TIME
10–15 minutes

Salt and freshly ground
black pepper

1kg (2lb 3oz) floury
or waxy potatoes
(unpeeled), cut into
1–2cm (½–¾in) cubes

100ml (3½fl oz) olive oil

4 cloves of garlic, peeled
and crushed or finely
grated

2 tbsp chopped thyme
leaves

* Fill a large saucepan with water, add a pinch of salt and bring to the boil. Tip in the potatoes and cook for 2–5 minutes (floury potatoes will cook faster) until they have slightly softened, then drain before tipping onto kitchen paper to dry completely.

* Pour the olive oil into a large frying pan over a high heat and, when hot, add the potatoes and cook, tossing frequently, for 3–4 minutes or until they begin to turn a light golden colour. Add the garlic and thyme and cook for a further 3–5 minutes or until the potatoes are golden and crispy. Season with salt and pepper and serve immediately, or keep warm (uncovered to prevent them softening) until ready to serve.

Variations

Add 200g (7oz) diced bacon or pancetta to the frying pan at the same time as the potatoes.

Add the grated zest of 1 lemon at the same time as the garlic and thyme.

Add 2 teaspoons each of ground cumin and coriander instead of the thyme.

Add 1 teaspoon each of garam masala (to make your own, see page 129) and cayenne pepper instead of the garlic and thyme.

New potato salad

Fresh new potatoes are one of the seasonal foods I most look forward to each year. They need little more than a knob of butter to enhance them, but they're also great made into a salad. Dress the potatoes while they are still warm so that they absorb the flavours in the dressing.

Serves 4 (v)

PREPARATION TIME
5 minutes

COOKING TIME
15–20 minutes

Salt and freshly ground black pepper

2 eggs (optional)

400g (14oz) new potatoes, left unpeeled and halved or quartered

2 tbsp capers, drained and rinsed

5 cornichons or 2 gherkins, cut into 5mm (¼in) thick slices

4 spring onions, trimmed and sliced

For the vinaigrette

3 tbsp olive oil

1 tbsp cider vinegar

1 tsp Dijon mustard

1 tbsp chopped tarragon

* Fill a large saucepan with water and add 1 teaspoon of salt with the eggs (if using) and potatoes. Bring to the boil, then cook the eggs for 10 minutes and use a slotted spoon to remove them. Leave the potatoes to cook for about another 5 minutes. While the potatoes finish cooking, run the eggs under cold water before peeling and setting aside.

* In a bowl, whisk together all the ingredients for the vinaigrette and season with salt and pepper.

* Drain the potatoes, then, while still warm, toss with the vinaigrette, capers, cornichons or gherkins and spring onions. Arrange the potato salad on plates, then cut the hard-boiled eggs into quarters and divide between the plates.

Paprika potato wedges

Paprika and potatoes are an irresistible combination that go well with roasted meats such as chicken.

Serves 4 (v)

PREPARATION TIME
5 minutes

COOKING TIME
25 minutes

50ml (2fl oz) olive oil

1 tsp smoked paprika

1 tsp caster sugar

1 tsp salt

650g (1lb 7oz) floury potatoes (peeled or unpeeled), each cut into 6 wedges

* Preheat the oven to 230°C (450°F), Gas mark 8.

* Pour the olive oil into a large bowl and add the paprika, sugar and salt. Mix together, then add the potatoes and toss well to coat.

* Tip the coated potato wedges into a roasting tin (making sure to include all the oil from the bowl) and spread out in a single layer. Roast for about 10 minutes, then remove from the oven and turn the potatoes over, returning to the oven to cook for a further 15 minutes or until golden and a little crunchy on the outside.

Fried kale

Kale comes in a number of varieties, including curly, red and the beautiful black leaf, also known by its Italian name, cavolo nero.

Serves 4–6 (v)

PREPARATION TIME
5 minutes

COOKING TIME
3–7 minutes

400g (14oz) (prepared weight) kale leaves, stalks and centre ribs removed and leaves shredded

50ml (2fl oz) olive oil

Salt and freshly ground black pepper

* If the kale leaves are large, you will need to blanch them first, otherwise they won't be tender enough. To do this, simply cook them in a saucepan of boiling water (with a good pinch of salt) on a high heat for 2–3 minutes or until just beginning to wilt, then drain.

* Next, fry the kale. Pour the olive oil into the saucepan, still on a medium heat and, when the oil is hot, add the kale. Season with salt and pepper and cook the kale for 3–4 minutes, tossing frequently, until lightly browned and sweet-smelling. Serve immediately.

Variation

Fried kale with oyster sauce: Stir 2 tablespoons of oyster sauce into the fried kale.

Root vegetable mash

For a variation on standard mashed potato, why not try making it with other root vegetables? This recipe uses a mixture of parsnip, celeriac and sweet potato for a luxurious mash that's full of flavour.

Serves 4–6 (v)

PREPARATION TIME
15 minutes

COOKING TIME
20–25 minutes

1 carrot, peeled and cut into 2cm (¾in) chunks

Salt and freshly ground black pepper

1 parsnip, peeled and cut into 2cm (¾in) chunks

½ celeriac, peeled and cut into 2cm (¾in) chunks

1 sweet new potato, peeled and cut into 2cm (¾in) chunks

25g (1oz) butter or 2 tbsp olive oil

25ml (1fl oz) double or regular cream (optional)

1 tbsp chopped parsley

1 tbsp chopped thyme or rosemary leaves

* Place the carrot in a large saucepan and cover with cold water, adding a good pinch of salt. Bring to the boil, then reduce the heat to medium–high and simmer for 5 minutes. Tip in the parsnip, celeriac and sweet potato and continue cooking for another 15 minutes or until all the vegetables are tender.

* Drain well, then add the butter or olive oil and the cream (if using). Mash the vegetables either by hand or in a food processor for a smoother purée. Taste for seasoning, adding pepper and more salt if needed, then stir in the chopped herbs and serve.

Red cabbage coleslaw

Coleslaw is the perfect salad to serve with barbecued meats, fried chicken and spicy ribs. This variation is a vibrant purple colour.

Serves 6–8 (v)

PREPARATION TIME
10 minutes

400g (14oz) red cabbage

1 large carrot, peeled and grated

1 red onion, peeled and finely sliced

1 stick of celery, trimmed and finely sliced

200ml (7fl oz) mayonnaise

Salt and freshly ground black pepper

* Chop the cabbage lengthways into quarters, then cut out the core and slice the leaves crossways into fine shreds, about 5mm (¼ in) thick.

* Place the cabbage in a large bowl, then add the remaining ingredients and mix together, seasoning to taste with salt and pepper.

Buttered cabbage

Cabbage is probably pork's best friend. Cooked for just a few minutes, no more, it is soft and sweet.

Serves 4–6 (v)

PREPARATION TIME
3 minutes

COOKING TIME
5 minutes

450g (1lb) cabbage, such as Savoy, tough outer leaves removed

25g (1oz) butter

Salt and freshly ground black pepper

* Chop the cabbage lengthways into quarters, then cut out the core and slice the leaves crossways into fine shreds, about 5mm (¼ in) thick.

* Place the butter and 2 tablespoons of water in a large saucepan on a medium heat and when the butter has melted, toss in the cabbage and stir to coat. Season with salt and pepper, cover with a lid and cook, stirring every now and then, for 2–3 minutes or until just softened. Taste for seasoning and serve.

Variation

Spicy buttered cabbage: Add ½ teaspoon of ground caraway seeds and a pinch of dried chilli flakes to the cabbage when it is cooking.

Roasted cauliflower with gremolata

Gremolata is an Italian condiment made from a mixture of garlic, parsley and lemon peel that is traditionally served with braised veal but is equally at home sprinkled over fish and provides a lovely tangy foil to roasted cauliflower, as here. By roasting cauliflower the florets take on a charred crispness while the flesh remains soft and yielding.

Serves 4–6 (v)

PREPARATION TIME
10 minutes

COOKING TIME
20 minutes

2 cauliflowers, cut into florets

110ml (4fl oz) olive oil

Salt and freshly ground black pepper

For the gremolata

Finely grated zest of 2 lemons

2 cloves of garlic, peeled and crushed or finely grated

4 tbsp finely chopped parsley

2 tsp olive oil

* Preheat the oven to 200°C (400°F), Gas mark 6.

* Place the cauliflower florets in a large bowl and mix with the olive oil, then season with salt and pepper. Place on a baking tray and roast in the oven for about 20 minutes, stirring halfway through the cooking time, until the cauliflower is tender and just browned at the edges.

* While the cauliflower is roasting, make the gremolata by simply mixing all the ingredients together and seasoning with salt and pepper to taste. When the cauliflower is cooked, lightly mix with the gremolata and serve.

Green beans with anchovies and toasted almonds

I sometimes like to dress up green beans with anchovies for an intense savoury flavour and almonds for extra crunch.

Serves 6–8

PREPARATION TIME
5 minutes

COOKING TIME
5 minutes

Salt and freshly ground black pepper

500g (1lb 2oz) green beans, topped and tailed

50g (2oz) flaked almonds

10 tinned anchovies, chopped

2 tbsp olive oil

* Fill a saucepan with water, add a pinch of salt and bring to the boil, then tip in the green beans and cook for 2–3 minutes or until just tender.

* While the beans cook, toast the almonds in a small frying pan on a high heat and cook, tossing frequently, for 1 minute or until browned, then transfer to a bowl and mix together with the anchovies and olive oil. When the beans are cooked, drain, then toss in the bowl with the anchovies and toasted almonds. Serve while warm.

Sautéed courgettes

These courgettes are cooked for just a few minutes to retain a little bite. They make a perfect accompaniment to chicken or fish.

Serves 4 (v)

PREPARATION TIME
3 minutes

COOKING TIME
2–3 minutes

6 tbsp olive oil

2 courgettes, cut into 1cm (½in) cubes or slices at an angle

Salt and freshly ground black pepper

* Pour the olive oil into a frying pan on a high heat and when the oil is hot add the courgettes. Season with salt and pepper, then sauté for 2–3 minutes, tossing regularly, or until just softened. Serve immediately.

Variation

Sautéed courgettes with herbs: Try stirring in 1 tablespoon of chopped mint or basil with the cooked courgettes.

Broccoli and oyster sauce

Oyster sauce really complements greens such as broccoli. The combination works with any Chinese-style meat dish.

Serves 4–6 (v) **if using vegetarian oyster sauce**

PREPARATION TIME
5 minutes

COOKING TIME
5 minutes

1 tbsp sunflower oil

2 cloves of garlic, peeled and finely sliced

1 head of broccoli, cut into florets

3 tbsp oyster sauce or vegetarian oyster sauce

1 tbsp soy sauce

* Pour the sunflower oil into a frying pan on a medium–high heat and, when hot, stir in the garlic and broccoli.

* Cook, stirring occasionally, for 3 minutes, then add 100ml (3½ fl oz) water, cover with a lid and cook for a further 3 minutes or until the broccoli is just tender. Stir in the oyster and soy sauces, then remove from the heat and serve.

Sticky roast carrots in maple syrup

Maple syrup enhances the sweetness in carrots. Serve with Honey Mustard Pork Chops or Tarragon Chicken (pages 189 and 184).

Serves 4 (v)

PREPARATION TIME
5 minutes

COOKING TIME
35–40 minutes

500g (1lb 2oz) carrots

4 tbsp maple syrup

2 tbsp olive oil

Salt and freshly ground black pepper

* Preheat the oven to 220°C (425°F), Gas mark 7.

* Peel the carrots, then cut in half lengthways and slice at an angle into 4–5cm (1½–2in) lengths.

* In a bowl, toss all the ingredients together and season with salt and pepper. Tip out on a roasting tin, spreading out in a single layer, then place in the oven and roast, tossing once or twice, for 35–40 minutes or until sticky and lightly scorched.

Two ways with lentils

The lentils in these recipes are substantial enough to be eaten on their own, but they also go well with meat, especially pork or game.

Simple lentils

300g (11oz) Puy lentils

1 onion, peeled and halved

1 sprig of rosemary or thyme

1 bay leaf

Salt and freshly ground black pepper

2 tbsp olive oil

1 tsp balsamic vinegar

Serves 4 (v)

PREPARATION TIME
2 minutes

COOKING TIME
25–30 minutes

* Place the lentils in a saucepan with the onion, herbs and bay leaf. Pour in 1 litre (1¾ pints) water and bring to the boil, then reduce the heat and simmer, uncovered, for 20–25 minutes or until the lentils are tender.

* Drain the lentils, discarding the onion, herbs and bay leaf. Season with salt and pepper, then stir in the olive oil and balsamic vinegar to serve.

Substantial lentils

2 tbsp olive oil

1 onion, peeled and finely chopped

1 carrot, peeled and finely chopped

1 stick of celery, peeled and finely chopped

2 cloves of garlic, peeled and finely chopped

250g (9oz) Puy lentils

500ml (18fl oz) vegetable or chicken stock

1 sprig of thyme

1 bay leaf

Salt and freshly ground black pepper

Serves 4 (v, if using vegetable stock)

PREPARATION TIME
10 minutes

COOKING TIME
30–35 minutes

* Pour the olive oil into a saucepan on a medium heat and, when hot, stir in the onion, carrot, celery and garlic. Cover with a lid and cook for 6–8 minutes or until the vegetables are softened.

* Add the lentils, stock, thyme and bay leaf. Bring to the boil, then reduce the heat and simmer, uncovered, for 20–25 minutes or until the lentils are tender and the stock absorbed. Remove the herbs, add seasoning and serve.

Plain boiled rice

To achieve perfectly fluffy boiled rice, rinse the uncooked rice really well and boil it in water. You can add various spices or fresh herbs once it has been cooked – see the variations below.

Serves 4 (v)

PREPARATION TIME
2 minutes

COOKING TIME
10–15 minutes

225g (8oz) basmati rice
Good pinch of salt

* Place the rice in a sieve and rinse under cold running water until the water runs clear. Tip the rice into a saucepan, add 350ml (12fl oz) water and season with the salt. Bring to the boil, then reduce the heat to very low.

* Cover the pan with a lid and simmer for 10–15 minutes or until the rice is tender and all the water has been absorbed, only removing the lid briefly during cooking to check on the rice. Take off the heat and use a fork to fluff up the grains of rice before serving.

Variations

Whole spices are a great way of adding flavour to plain boiled rice. Try adding one or two of the following during cooking: a short 2.5cm (1in) stick of cinnamon, 3–4 green cardamom pods, 1 whole star anise, 2 whole cloves.

I also like to stir fresh herbs, such as 2 tablespoons of chopped coriander or parsley into the cooked rice.

Brown pilaf rice

Brown rice grains retain their outer shell, so take longer to cook than white rice. It has a nuttier flavour and slightly toothier texture.

Serves 4
(v, if using vegetable stock)

PREPARATION TIME
5 minutes

COOKING TIME
40–45 minutes

200g (7oz) brown basmati rice

25g (1oz) butter

1 onion, peeled and finely chopped

2 cloves of garlic, peeled and finely sliced

550ml (19fl oz) vegetable or chicken stock

Salt and freshly ground black pepper

* Place the rice in a sieve and rinse under cold running water until the water runs clear.

* Melt the butter in a saucepan over a medium heat and, when foaming, add the onion and garlic. Cover with a lid and sweat for 6–8 minutes or until softened but not browned.

* Tip in the rice and stir-fry for 1 minute, then pour in the stock. Season with salt and pepper, then bring to the boil, reduce the heat to medium–low, cover with a lid and cook for 30–35 minutes or until the stock has been absorbed and the rice is tender. Use a fork to fluff up the grains of rice before serving.

Couscous

Couscous takes only minutes to prepare. Its gorgeous flavour and texture goes well in salads and with many meat and fish dishes.

Serves 4
(v, if using vegetable stock)

PREPARATION TIME
2 minutes

COOKING TIME
5 minutes, plus soaking

400ml (14fl oz) vegetable or chicken stock

300g (11oz) couscous

4 tbsp olive oil

1 tbsp chopped parsley

Salt and freshly ground black pepper

* Pour the stock into a large saucepan and bring to the boil, then stir in the couscous and olive oil, remove from the heat and allow to stand for 5–6 minutes or until all the stock has been absorbed.

* Use a fork to fluff up the grains of couscous, then stir in the herbs, season with salt and pepper and serve.

Brown scones with treacle and sesame seeds

Two of my favourite ways of eating these sweet, wholemeal scones are toasted, buttered and drizzled with honey or served with cheese and pickles.

Makes 10–12 scones (v)

PREPARATION TIME
15 minutes

COOKING TIME
15–20 minutes

225g (8oz) plain flour, plus extra for dusting

225g (8oz) wholemeal flour

1 tsp salt

1 tsp bicarbonate of soda

25g (1oz) sesame seeds, plus extra for sprinkling (optional)

25g (1oz) butter, diced

1 egg

400ml (14fl oz) buttermilk or soured milk (add 2 tsp vinegar or lemon juice to 400ml (14fl oz) cow's milk or soy or rice milk and leave to stand for 10–15 minutes)

1 tbsp black treacle

* Preheat the oven to 220°C (425°F), Gas mark 7. Dust a baking sheet with flour.

* Put the wholemeal, plain flour and salt into a large bowl. Sift in the bicarbonate of soda and stir in the sesame seeds. Using your fingertips, rub in the butter until the mixture resembles coarse breadcrumbs.

* In a separate bowl, whisk the egg with the buttermilk or soured milk, then stir in the treacle and pour most of the liquid into the dry ingredients. Using one hand with your fingers held out like a claw, mix in full circles to bring the flour and liquid together, adding more liquid if necessary. The dough should be quite soft, but not too sticky.

* Turn the dough out onto a lightly floured work surface and gently bring it together into a ball, but without kneading it, then flatten it slightly to about 3cm (1¼ in) high. Cut the dough into 10–12 square or round scones. If you like, you can brush the tops of the scones with any leftover liquid and sprinkle with some extra sesame seeds.

* Put the scones onto the prepared baking sheet and pop in the oven to bake for 15–20 minutes (depending on the size of the scones). Have a look at them after 10 minutes: if they're already a deep golden brown, then turn the heat down to 200°C (400°F), Gas mark 6, for the remainder of the cooking time. When cooked they should sound hollow when tapped on the base. Transfer to a wire rack to cool.

Poppy seed scones

Tiny poppy seeds have a distinctive nutty flavour that complement all sorts of baked goods, from bread to cakes and scones. These scones are great served with butter and jam for breakfast or with a big bowl of warming soup.

Makes 10–12 scones (v)

PREPARATION TIME
15 minutes

COOKING TIME
12–15 minutes

450g (1lb) plain flour, plus extra for dusting

1 tsp salt

½ tsp bicarbonate of soda

25g (1oz) poppy seeds

400ml (14fl oz) buttermilk or soured milk (add 2 tsp vinegar or lemon juice to 400ml (14fl oz) cow's milk or soy or rice milk and leave to stand for 10–15 minutes)

* Preheat the oven to 230°C (450°F), Gas mark 8. Dust a baking sheet with flour.

* Sift the flour, salt and bicarbonate of soda into a large bowl and stir in the poppy seeds. Rub the mixture with your fingertips to incorporate some air, then make a well in the centre and pour in most of the buttermilk or soured milk. Using one hand with your fingers held out like a claw, mix in full circles to bring the flour and liquid together, adding more liquid if necessary. The dough should be quite soft, but not too sticky.

* Turn the dough out onto a lightly floured work surface and gently bring it together into a ball, but without kneading it, then flatten it slightly to about 3cm (1¼ in) high. Cut the dough into 10–12 round or square scones, each about 6cm (2½ in) across, then place on the prepared baking sheet. If you like, you can brush the tops of the scones with any leftover liquid.

* Pop in the oven and bake for 12–15 minutes (depending on the size of the scones). Have a look at them after 10 minutes: if they are already a deep golden brown, then turn the heat down to 200°C (400°F), Gas mark 6, for the remainder of the cooking time. When cooked they should sound hollow when tapped on the base. Transfer to a wire rack to cool.

Quick red pepper and pesto focaccia

Though not strictly a real focaccia, this quick version (using bicarbonate of soda instead of yeast) is nonetheless full of flavour. It is a fantastic accompaniment to pasta dishes or just eaten in chunks fresh from the oven. One tip when making it: don't be shy with the olive oil.

Makes 8 slices (v)

PREPARATION TIME
10 minutes

COOKING TIME
30 minutes

50–75ml (2–3fl oz) extra-virgin olive oil

450g (1lb) plain flour, plus extra for dusting

1 tsp salt

½ tsp bicarbonate of soda

350–400ml (12–14fl oz) buttermilk or soured milk (add 2 tsp vinegar or lemon juice to 400ml (14fl oz) cow's milk or soy or rice milk and leave to stand for 10–15 minutes)

100g (3½oz) preserved roasted red peppers (from a jar or tin), cut into 1cm (½in) pieces

1 tbsp pesto

Good pinch of sea salt

20 x 30cm (8 x 12in) Swiss roll tin or roasting tin

* Preheat the oven to 230°C (450°F), Gas mark 8. Brush the tin very generously with about half the olive oil (more than you think you will need).

* Sift the flour, salt and bicarbonate of soda into a large bowl, and make a well in the centre. Pour in most of the buttermilk or soured milk, then stir in the red peppers and pesto.

* Using one hand with your fingers held out like a claw, mix in the flour from the sides of the bowl, adding more milk if necessary. The dough should be softish, but not too wet and sticky. When it all comes together, turn it out onto a floured work surface and roll it out so that it will fit on the prepared tin. Transfer the dough to the tin, generously drizzle more olive oil over the top and make some dimples over the surface with your fingertips. Sprinkle with the sea salt.

* Bake in the oven for about 30 minutes or until the bread is golden both on top and underneath. If it seems to be browning too quickly, turn the oven down to 200°C (400°F), Gas mark 6 after 10 or 15 minutes.

* When the focaccia is cooked but still hot, drizzle just a little more olive oil over the top. Transfer to a wire rack to cool slightly before serving.

Shortbread biscuits

These melt-in-the-mouth biscuits are perfect served with a morning or afternoon cup of tea or to accompany light desserts such as the Apple Fool (page 199), Lemon Posset (page 201) or Chocolate Zabaglione (page 207).

Makes 15–20 biscuits (v)

PREPARATION TIME
10 minutes

COOKING TIME
6–10 minutes

150g (5oz) plain flour, plus extra for dusting

100g (3½oz) butter, softened and diced

50g (2oz) caster sugar

* Preheat the oven to 180°C (350°F), Gas mark 4.

* Sift the flour into a large bowl and, using your fingertips, rub in the butter until the mixture resembles fine breadcrumbs. Add the sugar and bring the whole mixture together to form a stiff dough. (Don't be tempted to add any water.) Alternatively, briefly mix the ingredients in a food processor until they come together.

* Transfer the dough to a lightly floured work surface and roll out to about 5mm (¼ in) thick. Cut into rounds, fingers, squares, dinosaurs or whatever shape takes your fancy, then lift carefully onto a prepared baking sheet with a palette knife or fish slice, spacing the biscuits evenly apart.

* Bake for 6–10 minutes or until pale golden, then remove from the oven and allow to cool on the baking sheet for a minute or so before carefully transferring to a wire rack to cool down completely.

Variations

Sift in one of the following to the flour: 1 teaspoon of ground ginger or ground cinnamon or 2 tablespoons of cocoa powder.

Add the finely grated zest of 1 orange or 1 lemon with the caster sugar.

Index

Acknowledgements

I'm so very grateful for all the help and support I received from the many people involved in the creation of this book. Everybody at Collins, especially the indefatigable Jenny Heller and her amazing team: Georgina Atsiaris, Emma Callery, Kate Parker, Kathy Steer, Martin Topping, Heike Schuessler, Andrew Cunning, Myfanwy Vernon-Hunt and William Ricketts; also Philip Webb, Heather Favell, Joss Herd, Bridget Sargeson, Jo Harris, Lorna Brash, Helen Walsh and Mark Cook.

Thanks so much to my agents at Limelight Management: Fiona Lindsay, Mary Bekhait, Alison Lindsay and Maclean Lindsay and also to Diarmaid Falvey, Conor Pyne, David Nottage from Sweet Productions, Brian Walsh from RTE, and everybody at the Good Food Channel.

At home a very big heartfelt thanks to my husband Isaac and my assistant Josh Heller who both worked by my side on this book . Great help came from Thomas Smiddy too and also Bree Allen (thanks for inviting Scarlett over to play nearly every day!), Miriam Hartmann, Friederike Stein and Susan Mannio. And huge thanks to Irish fashion designer Lucy Downes for her finest quality cashmere (www.sphereone.ie).

Which brings me to Ballymaloe. Thank you to all the wonderful staff and family both at the cookery school and at Ballymaloe House – from the gardens and farm right through to the dining room. It's amazing to think that the whole thing started back in 1964 with a small ad in a local newspaper inviting people to "dine in a country house", and the lady who wrote that is to whom I dedicate this book; Myrtle Allen.

This edition produced for The Book People Ltd
Hall Wood Avenue, Haydock, St Helens WA11 9UL

First published in 2011 by Collins, an imprint of
HarperCollinsPublishers

77-85 Fulham Palace Road
Hammersmith
London, W6 8JB
www.harpercollins.co.uk

10 9 8 7 6 5 4 3 2 1

A catalogue record of this book is available from the British Library

ISBN 978-0-00-790524-9

Printed and bound in Italy by Lego
Publishing Director – Jenny Heller
Design – Martin Topping and Myfanwy Vernon-Hunt
Illustration – William Ricketts
Senior Project Editor – Georgina Atsiaris
Editors – Emma Callery, Kate Parker and Kathy Steer
Production Controller – Stuart Masheter
Food styling – Joss Herd, Bridget Sargeson and Lorna Brash
Prop styling – Jo Harris

FSC is a non-profit international organisation to promote the responsible management of
the world's forests. Products carrying the FSC label are independently certified to assure
consumers that they come from forests that are managed to meet the social, economic and
ecological needs of present and future generations.

Find out more about HarperCollins and the environment at www.harpercollins.co.uk/green